Ask
SUPERNANNY

Jo Frost

What Every Parent Wants to Know

HYPERION

A BIG BIG THANK YOU

To everybody involved in the Supernanny Project UK/USA
for another year of such dedicated work.

To all the families who have touched my life throughout filming in the UK and USA –
your courage has inspired millions worldwide. Stand proud.

To my family and friends who have listened to me talk the
hind legs off a donkey whilst filming and never failed to throw back lots
of love and humor when the going got tough – xx.

To "Big Man," from the beginning – xx.

To Liz Wilhide – we've made a good team.

DEDICATION

This book is dedicated to my grandparents, Fran and Dick, and Isabella
and Nathan, for the fondest memories I hold as an adult growing up.

Love always, Joanne xx

Copyright © 2006 Channel 4
Photographs copyright © Mark Read

First published in Great Britain in 2006 by Hodder and Stoughton
A division of Hodder Headline

SUPERNANNY is a trademark of, and is licensed by, Ricochet Productions Limited

Props kindly supplied by Early Learning Centre www.elc.co.uk
and Mamas & Papas www.mamasandpapas.co.uk

ISBN: 1-4013-0864-3

Hyperion books are available for special promotions and premiums.
For details contact Michael Rentas, Assistant Director, Inventory Operations, Hyperion,
77 West 66th Street, 12th floor, New York, New York 10023, or call 212-456-0133.

FIRST HYPERION EDITION

10 9 8 7 6 5 4 3 2 1

Contents

Introduction 6

1 Family Dynamics 10
2 Mealtimes 52
3 Bedtimes 76
4 Home and Away 108
5 Stuff Happens 148
6 The Naughty Step and Beyond 168
7 Positive Feedback 198

Useful contacts 220
Index 222

Introduction

This introduction gives me the perfect opportunity to thank the millions of you worldwide who have watched *Supernanny*, and the families here in Britain and in the United States who have been courageous enough to take part and make it happen. It has been an amazing success and even now, two years on, I still find myself in bewilderment at the whirlwind of it all.

I know from the thousands of emails, letters, and phone calls I've received that my work on the show has been truly inspirational to many parents who find themselves faced with the same issues I solve on the program. Some have seen a reflection of their own family life while they were watching the show, decided to take positive action, and have gone on to achieve success, changing the hand they thought they had no choice but to live with. That's why I love doing what I do!

When I visit a family, I spend the first day observing their interactions with each other in their own living environment. It's then that I get the chance to see what lies at the root of the problems they're facing on the surface. Untangling these issues can be very complex, like working out a really difficult puzzle, but it's only by peeling back the layers that I find the hidden story that lies beneath.

For all of you out there who want to try my techniques, *Ask Supernanny* provides the answers that you want to know. The questions featured in this book come from my mailbag as well as from my website, www.b4ugo-ga-ga.co.uk, and cover a whole range of issues. I know problems can crop up in different areas, but to avoid repetition, I've focused on key areas of difficulty and arranged the questions – and my answers – by theme.

I've also included my own A–Z. As parents, you embark upon a journey, a long and fruitful one. There will be the chance to sightsee at beauty spots along the way, but sometimes you'll hit a dead end. To avoid taking too many wrong turns, look out for my navigational tips on keeping positive. "Are we there yet, Mommy?" "No, darling, this is just the beginning . . ."

A positive approach to parenting is the ONLY way to ensure that your children get the love and guidance they need. Your acknowledgment of their achievements gives them confidence in what they strive to do, and a healthy mental attitude they take into adulthood.

As adults we express ourselves freely, sometimes even loosely, to those we know best, expecting them to be able to read between the lines if necessary. For children, this is something they only learn to develop over time. Kids hear the inflection in our voices, the words we say, and take it literally. After all, why shouldn't they?

Some of the work I do with families on the show is about teaching them better communication skills. Learning to listen is a major one! Your young ones will look up to *you* as parents – so take responsibility for your actions and keep talking and listening to your children. In the same way, a lot of times when I see parents struggling with a technique, the problem is that they've left out a step or acted inconsistently. It may not seem a big deal to adults, but to a child it can make all the difference.

Before a baby is born, most people have an idealized view of the kind of parent they want to be. Nine times out of ten I hear the word "perfect" – what exactly is perfect? Raising children is about making a personal commitment – and sometimes sacrifices – along the way.

But I can tell you very confidently that all parents learn as they go along. When you make a wrong decision, it's up to you to learn from it and make a better judgment next time. You only make mistakes if you keep going over the same old ground without changing the outcome.

Fear of failure and fear of ridicule are two of the biggest obstacles I see parents face. FEAR FEAR FEAR. It's a real blocker, it's negative energy, and it sets parents up for failure. Usually fear comes from not knowing what the outcome of a situation will be, and from lack of confidence and courage. Lack of support can make it worse. When parents feel like that, they think it's easier to ignore problems and hope they will go away eventually. But taking a backseat in your own family life leads to the chaos I walk into on *Supernanny*.

"The No-nonsense Nanny" is how the press have described me. "She doesn't mince her words." Honestly, I just don't see the point in doing otherwise. I want parents to get results, not exhaust themselves avoiding problems. Honesty is a good foundation to build on. It leaves plenty of room for trust, respect, and close relationships with your children. If that means upsetting the apple

cart at times, so be it. What I do know is that honesty gives parents a clean slate so they can pull together, present a united front to get their family back on track, and remind themselves of their strengths and blessings. Like my father would say: "Joanne, that's why we were made with our eyes at the front of our heads and not the back, so we can look forward and never look behind." How true that is, although after looking after children for more than sixteen years, I sometimes wish I had an extra pair!

"Can I take a picture of you so I can scare my daughter and tell her that I know you?" "Yes, we may be on a cruise ship, but Supernanny's black cab can fly, you know." "I have Supernanny's number and Daddy will call her if you carry on." "Santa Claus listens to Supernanny." "Mommy knows Supernanny, so behave."

Apparently I have become the new bogeyman for some of you out there. So, that only leaves me with one more thing to say – I think it's time you parents were given the tools to be Supermommy and Superdaddy yourselves! Get reading, take back the reins, and be in control of your wonderful family life. After all, it is what *you* make it.

ENJOY! xx

1 Family Dynamics

The first thing I do when I visit a family is take a backseat and observe what's going on. I watch the family dynamics, right from first thing in the morning to the last thing at night. I watch how the parents relate to each other and how they engage with their kids, and make a mental note of the problem areas and which parts of family life are running more smoothly. Although I might ask a few questions at this stage, I don't really comment and I rarely intervene unless it's absolutely necessary. I'm just there as an observer of the family dynamic – a fly on the wall.

Many of the families we feature on *Supernanny* are aware of their difficulties. What they may not have been able to see is what triggers certain kinds of behavior in their kids. Sometimes they are just too locked into a particular pattern that is not serving them or their children very well, to be able to see a way out of it. Or there may be several issues going on outside the home that distort the picture. My role as an outside observer is first to spot the behavior patterns and then to show parents the many different ways of tackling their problems so they can resolve them together.

When you're stretched every day as a parent, juggling different demands on your time, it can be difficult to step back and see the big picture. Things aren't always black and white. It's often hard to identify the real root of a problem, as opposed to its secondary or added-on effects. I sometimes find that parents single out one child's behavior as the source of their problems, or identify one part of their lives – mealtimes, for example, or

getting to school on time – as the main area of difficulty. This may well be a true reflection of what's going on – the toddler may be ruling the roost, or mealtimes might be complete and utter chaos. But it's often more complicated than that.

Kids who find it difficult to get going in the morning, for example, may be overtired. You can encourage them to be better organized and more self-sufficient, but if they're not getting enough sleep because they're going to bed too late and getting out of bed too often, the problem really starts the night before. And sometimes it's just too easy to lay all the blame for a family's problems on the child who's constantly getting into trouble day after day. Instead of focusing on that child and what he's doing, to the exclusion of everything else, looking at the family dynamic as a whole often suggests reasons why that child is so desperate for attention that he is trying everything in the book, and then some, just to get noticed. Once you see and understand what's behind the behavior, you're halfway there.

It takes a lot of courage to invite a television crew into your lives and open your family life up to millions of viewers. It takes even more courage to change, to admit mistakes, and move on – which isn't as easy as some people might think! I've got nothing but respect and admiration for all the families who have agreed to take part in *Supernanny* and go through that learning curve in public. These families have truly been an inspiration for viewers around the world. From the feedback I receive, I know that many of those viewers now feel empowered to try to achieve the same goals themselves.

You do not need to share your life with a TV crew to benefit from the techniques I use on the series. But the techniques will work much better if you first spend a little time looking at the patterns in your own family dynamic. That way you will begin to get an idea of the overall picture and see how change in one area might lead to improvements in other parts of your life – improvements that you might not even have expected.

Topics and techniques covered in this chapter:

ASSESSING YOUR FAMILY DYNAMIC to identify strengths and weaknesses

CREATING A ROUTINE and routines for families where both parents work

SAME-PAGE TECHNIQUE for positive communication between parents

ONE-IN-THREE TECHNIQUE to help parents resolve their differences

TRADING-TASKS TECHNIQUE to help parents share the workload

STEP-UP/STEP-BACK TECHNIQUE to help parents share the workload

HOW TO TALK TO YOUR CHILD – the three essential voices

MOVING ON and leaving traumatic events behind

SINGLE PARENTING and how to cope

GRANDPARENTS and the "special relationship"

TWINS AND MULTIPLE BIRTHS – how to juggle the demands

A is for Acceptance.
Life deals us all sorts of cards. Accept what you can't change and move on.

Assessing your family dynamic

All families have their strengths and weaknesses. What are yours? Take a step back. Imagine going to the theater and sitting in the front row. Your family – right now, right here – is the play. What do you see? How does it make you feel? What makes you cringe with embarrassment? What makes you burst with pride? What makes you laugh? What makes you cry?

Keep a diary over a period of a week or two. Note the good things that happen as well as the problems: "Monday. 8.30 a.m. Rosie got dressed without making a fuss. Friday. 5.30 p.m. Ben pushed Rosie over when I was making supper, and wouldn't say sorry." Then run through the Assessment Checklist to help you identify which are your family's strengths and which are the areas where things could be better.

ASSESSMENT CHECKLIST:

1 Routine

Think about an average day. Do you have a routine, or set times for doing things, or is it more of a free-for-all? Do you find it difficult to get everything done that needs to be done?

When do you regularly feel pressed for time? Is it hard to give the kids breakfast and get them dressed, washed, and out of the house in time for school? In that case, have you got enough time between waking and leaving the house? Or is something else causing the problem – a "faddy" dresser, for instance, who can't decide what to wear, or a fussy eater who's working his way through every brand of cereal in the supermarket?

Think about an average week. You might take your toddler to playgroup on Tuesday afternoons, for example, or go to the supermarket every Saturday morning. Your older children may have regular activities or playdates after school. Are some days a whirlwind of activity, when you can barely catch your breath? Could you shop on another day or move a playdate to take the pressure off?

Are you bored with your routine? Are your kids? Could you utilize your time and management skills to bring more balance and variety into your family life?

Some parents fill every minute of the day with activities for their children – outings, music lessons, football practice, choir – with the result that their kids become overloaded and never get the chance to unwind and learn how to entertain themselves. Others allow so much unstructured free time that their kids get bored and start to squabble or get into mischief. Somewhere between these two extremes is the balance you should aim for.

2 Trouble spots

When you're right in the thick of things, separating fighting siblings every two minutes, or dealing with your toddler's round-the-clock tantrums, it's easy to lose your perspective. This is where a diary comes in handy. Refer back to it to see when and where problems tend to occur. Can you see a pattern emerging? Are there underlying issues that never get resolved?

If your kids squabble, bicker, or fight, what sets them off? Is sharing an issue? Are certain toys regularly fought over? Do your kids always act up when you're otherwise occupied – on the phone, when friends come around for a chat, when you're trying to talk to your partner? How do your kids behave outside the home?

The timing of outbursts can also be very revealing. When are your kids more likely to quarrel? When is your toddler most likely to have a meltdown? Small children who lose it just before lunch or just before the evening meal may well be hungry. Low blood sugar can make otherwise easygoing kids irritable. Bringing your mealtimes forward a little can help to ease the situation. In the same way, kids who are fractious in the evening may be overtired. An earlier bedtime could be the answer.

3 You and your partner

Do you and your partner share the same style of parenting? Do you agree about what your children are allowed to do and what they are not allowed to do? Do you share the same attitude toward discipline, or is one of you stricter than the other? On which points do you differ? On what points do you agree?

Do you ever air your differences in front of your children? If you tell your son he can't watch any more TV, does he then go and see if Dad will let him? And does he?

Which one of you is more likely to be listened to? Which one of you finds it more difficult to set boundaries and tends to let things slide? Be honest. Who's the pushover? Who's the disciplinarian?

When it comes to looking after the children, who does what? Do you both take turns whenever you can, or does most of the responsibility fall on one parent? What happens on weekends? Is it any different?

How much free time do you have as a couple? How do you spend it – seeing friends or family, going out, watching TV? What do you miss most about your lives before you had children? What do you enjoy most about being parents?

4 Chores and housework

Make a list of household chores. Then note which ones you do, which ones your partner does, which you do together, and which, if any, the children help with.

Your list might include:

- Food shopping
- Preparing meals
- Setting the table
- Washing up
- General cleaning
- Tidying up
- Washing and ironing clothes
- Repairs and general maintenance
- Errands (taking the library books back, picking up the dry cleaning)
- Looking after pets (walking the dog, cleaning out the hamsters' cage)
- Gardening
- Washing the car
- Paying the bills and keeping track of household administration
- Organizing the kids' activities

Think about whether there are ways in which you could share the chores more equally between you and your partner. Think about ways you could teach your children to be more self-sufficient at their age. A five-year-old is not too young to set the table and may even be thrilled to help you, especially if you give him lots of praise. Prioritize the chores so you can keep on top of the important things.

Then think about the standards you set yourself. Are they too high – or not high enough? Would you rather tackle a backlog of ironing than sit down and play with your kids – or would it take a week's worth of cleaning up before you could face someone coming to your home?

5 Rewards and discipline

How often do you notice when your children are behaving well? Do you tell them? Do you reward them? Do you show them love and affection? Do you cuddle up with your kids and have special times with them?

If you reward them, what type of rewards do you give: praise, a star on a star chart (or some other visual aid), a treat, a toy, an outing? Do you find yourself bribing your children to do things? Do you buy your child presents when you feel guilty for not spending more time with her, or to make up for a disappointment of some kind?

Which methods of discipline do you use? How often do you find yourself shouting at your children? How often do you lose your cool? Do you set a good example for your kids? If you are using a technique like the Naughty Step or Time Out, do you always follow through? When you tell your kids not to do something, do you explain why? Or do you just say: "Because I say so"?

Would you say your methods are working? Or do you find yourself telling your children off over and over again about the same things?

6 Outside the home

How often do you do things as a family outside the home? What type of outings do you enjoy? What type of outings do your children enjoy?

Has your children's behavior ever stopped you from taking them shopping, to a family restaurant, to a friend's house? Are there places where other families go that you just wouldn't take your children in case they might embarrass you and act up? What about special occasions like weddings, christenings, and birthday parties?

Are journeys difficult? How do your children behave on the way to school? Or in the car? Or on the train to your mother's house?

7 Individual attention

How much time in the day does each child have for individual attention, one-to-one, from Mom or Dad or both? Does one child tend to get more attention than the others? Is that a result of bad behavior, or is it the result of age or need? Do you find it difficult to balance the time you spend looking after a baby or toddler with enough time for your older children?

A is for Attention.
Positive attention is a powerful way of reinforcing good behavior. Show your kids that you notice when they do well.

8 Support systems

How much support can you rely on to lighten the load? Do you belong to a babysitting circle? Do you go to playgroups? Is there a relative or friend you could call on for extra assistance – or simply to give you time to get out on your own or with your partner? Do you find it difficult to ask for help even when you're struggling? Do you think you should be responsible for everything and shouldn't need to ask for help?

9 Room for improvement

Write down the things you would most like to change about the way your family works. You might want to eat together as a family more often, or get through a meal without the children bickering or leaving the table leaving half their food untouched. You might want to share responsibilities more equally, or agree upon a shared approach to key issues with your partner. You might want to get on top of a bad behavior – lying, spitting, whining, hitting, whatever form it takes – for once and for all. Make a list of ten things you would change if you could.

It is important to be realistic. How do you measure what that is? Most goals are achievable; some are not. If the goals you set are possible and achievable, that's OK. If you make goals that are unattainable, you set yourself up for failure. Pressure on the family that comes from illness, disability, bereavement, financial difficulties, and other serious issues may be beyond your control. You will need to learn to accept and stop wasting time worrying about things you cannot change immediately. You can't

change a negative situation, but you can prevent it from having a negative impact. Every negative experience comes with a positive learning curve. But it's also important not to take things out of context. Are things really that bad?

10 Look to your strengths

Assessing your family dynamic isn't simply about pinpointing those problem areas you would like to work on and change. It's also about acknowledging what you do well so you learn to play to your true strengths. I'm not talking about making a superhuman effort or sacrificing one area of family life for another. I mean recognizing what you as a family do well.

Think about those times when everything seemed to run smoothly. What was going right? Were you and your partner more relaxed, less tired, or just in the mood to let down your hair and have fun with your kids? Write down ten things about your family that make you smile.

FAMILY MEETING

Have a family meeting and use the results of the Assessment Checklist to discuss things with your partner or with anyone else who is routinely involved in the care of your children. You may wish to review the checklist together. If there are points of disagreement, or if one parent is carrying too much of the load, you can use some of the techniques detailed later in this chapter, such as the Step-Up/Step-Back Technique (page 35) and the One-In-Three Technique (page 31), to help iron out your differences.

Q I really want to set up a routine like the ones I've seen on Supernanny. *Could you suggest a good framework for the day?*

A As you say, one of the first things I do on *Supernanny* is to put a workable routine in place for each family. This is written on a large sheet of paper and stuck up in a place where everyone in the family can see it and refer to it. It can also be written down in a diary, but having it on the wall means everyone can see what's supposed to be happening at any given time. You may also have noticed that every routine is different. That's because every family is different and has different needs. It's not one size fits all.

To sort out a schedule for yourself, you could start by writing down fixed points in the day for mealtimes. Meals are the cornerstone of any routine. There's a good reason for this. Delay a meal and your children's blood sugar levels will drop and they will become irritable, whiny, or uncooperative. Bring a meal too far forward and your children won't be hungry enough to eat what is set before them, which means that they will be begging for snacks between meals.

I'm in favor of an early evening meal for young kids – between 4:30 and 5:00 p.m. This allows enough time for a calm wind-down to bed. In my experience, a relatively early bedtime of between 7:00 and 7:30 p.m. is also good for small children. Children of school age can stay up to about 8:00 p.m.; once they're in secondary school, that can be made later.

As far as the other end of the day is concerned, be sure you allow enough time between waking up and getting out of the house to go to school – time to fit in washing and dressing, and eating breakfast. If you start off rushed, you'll set off on the wrong foot and the rest of the day will feel pressured. And your kids will have no time to practice those life skills, like getting dressed by themselves, which they need to learn.

Once you have decided a time for breakfast and the evening meal, you can fix a time for lunch at a sensible point in between. You might also want to set times for mid-morning and mid-afternoon snacks.

A basic framework might look like this:

Parents	Child 1	Child 2	Child 3
Getting up			
Breakfast			
Play/activity/nap*			
Mid-morning snack			
Play/activity/nap*			
Lunch			
Play/activity/nap*			
Mid-afternoon snack			
Play/activity/nap*			
Evening meal			
Bath			
Bedtime			

(*depending on the age of the child)

Now go back and try to fill in as much detail as you can. If you have a baby, how often does she need feeding, and how long do you feed her for? What are her sleep patterns during the day? How often does she wake up in the night? If you have small children, when do you give them their naps, and for how long? If your children are going to school, when do you leave in the morning, and return to pick them up in the afternoon? When do you set aside time for them to do their homework?

If your children don't go to school yet, make sure you prioritize times for their mental and physical development. Schedule different times for different sorts of play – quiet, managed play with games and puzzles; pretend play; and fun outdoors to let off steam and get some fresh air. Vary the activities throughout the day: Children get bored doing the same things all the time.

Your routine should also include set times for each child in the family to have one-on-one attention from a parent. It might be a special playtime, a story, an outing, or simply a supervised bath and bedtime. Rotate these between each parent. The length of time you spend with each child will vary according to the child's age. While you have one-on-one time with one child, set the other child up with an activity to focus on.

Just as important, you should also set aside times when you and your partner can enjoy some quality time together *without* your children. In most families, this will tend to be later on in the evening when the children have gone to bed, or on weekends when you can leave them with a babysitter.

And don't forget to make some space in the day when you can spend time on yourself – for a rest, a bath, an uninterrupted chat on the phone, or to read a book in peace. Of course, you can't simply leave young children to their own devices and put your feet up when you feel like it. But you can nap when they nap. Quality time is the first thing that drops out of the picture when a family is under pressure, but these periods are essential. The whole point of a routine is to utilize your time efficiently so that everyone's needs – including yours – are met.

The last thing to bear in mind is that a routine will always evolve. Children grow and develop very quickly. You will need to keep adjusting the times and activities as you go along to keep in step with the changing needs of the family, physical and emotional.

Tip: Recharge the batteries

Make sure you and your child get enough sleep, and recharge those batteries. A rested child is a receptive child.

Q *I'm not sure I really agree with the whole idea of sticking to a routine day after day. Isn't it a bit boring for the kids as well as for me? I like to be more spontaneous with my time. One of the reasons I enjoy being at home looking after my children is that I don't have to put up with the kind of rigid routine I had to follow when I was working in an office, week in week out.*

A Routines don't have to be dull, boring, or rigid. They are what you make of them. The main purpose of a routine is to give structure and shape to the day and make life easier. You'll have more opportunity to have fun *with* a routine in place than you would without it. Routines give families breathing space – and they should be flexible enough so you can tweak them here and there when you need to.

Small children benefit from a routine because they feel more secure. By contrast, when basically anything could happen at any time, they become unsettled. A structure allows them to know what's coming next and makes them more cooperative. But it also allows you to be more creative with your time so that you provide your children (and yourself) with a variety of different options to eliminate boredom.

For example, look at the way a good nursery or day-care center breaks down the day. There will be set times for arrival, snacks, lunch, washing, changing, naps, and departure. But there will also be times set aside for different kinds of play: indoor play (puzzles and games, role play, and nature study), creative play (building blocks, modeling, painting, and drawing), shared activities (stories, songs, and dancing), and outdoor play (climbing, running, and outdoor games). A structure or routine ensures that there is a good balance between quiet times and lively times, between mental and physical stimulation, and between activities that allow a child to develop as an individual and those that teach him social skills and an awareness of others.

B is for Boundaries.
Boundaries aren't barriers, they're safe limits within which kids can explore and develop. Put the boundaries in place so your children know what's expected of them.

Q *We set up a timetable for our family to follow, but it broke down after only a couple of days. What are we doing wrong – or is our life just too unpredictable to fit into a set schedule?*

A Life is unpredictable if you make it that way. It's important to know what you aim to achieve each day — otherwise life will be nerve-wracking for all concerned.

The first thing you have to ask yourself is whether you have been trying to follow the routine too rigidly. It's a framework; it doesn't have to be set in stone. Are you setting yourself up for failure? Are your goals impossible to achieve?

Provided you manage to keep mealtimes and bedtimes more or less in place, other events can shift around a bit — up to half an hour, say — without losing the benefit of a routine. Slackening the reins a little when you need to won't make a huge amount of difference.

Then ask yourself whether you have allocated your time realistically. If your child is a slow eater, have you allowed enough time for her to finish her food? Does she need more prompting and encouragement? If she finds it difficult to get going in the morning, have you set aside enough time for her to get ready for school? Within reason, work with what you've got.

Routines often fly out of the window because of unforeseen interruptions. But parents often forget they have a choice here. For example – and this is very common – if the phone rings at the time when you are putting your child down for a nap, *you don't*

have to answer it! It's what the answering machine is for. Even with a routine in place, there will be times when you have to think on your feet and be confident enough to make decisions and prioritize.

Routines also often fall apart because parents don't give them a chance. Do you communicate effectively with your children? You may know that it's almost time for the evening meal, but if you don't tell your kids, how are they supposed to know? "Supper in ten minutes." Give them a warning about what's going to happen next. "Supper in five minutes. Go and wash your hands, please." You need to be the Speaking Clock so that activities don't take your kids by surprise, and they can prepare themselves mentally for what's coming up next. Even older children will need reminding, particularly if they are stuck in a game or TV program and their attention is elsewhere.

Write the routine up on a big sheet of paper and stick it on the wall. I've found that once you do that, older kids often start to make reference to it because it makes them feel part of the whole picture. Then, as if by magic, they take responsibility for their days and start to get more involved. Some kids will even take the initiative and set out the knives and forks, for example, when they see that a mealtime's coming up.

Tip: Manage your time
Schedule events, such as deliveries, visits from friends, outings, and so on, around your routine so that you don't disrupt fixed points of the day unnecessarily. "Can I call you back in fifteen minutes?" That's a useful phrase to bear in mind.

Q We have three children, and my wife and I both work. Our two eldest are at school and the little one, Jamie, who's three, goes to nursery school. Can you suggest any ways we can make life less chaotic? There never seems to be enough time in the day – we spend more time in the car picking our kids up and dropping them off at different places than anything else. We've discussed the possibility of my wife giving up work for a while, but she enjoys her job and says she would be climbing the walls at home. I still can't help thinking that the kids might be better off if she could be persuaded to put her career on hold for a while.

A Some mothers want to stay at home, and that's great. Some decide that they will wait until their kids are in school before they go back to work, and that's fine, too. Some choose to go part-time, or work more flexibly, or work from home. Others have no choice but to go back to work, because the family needs two incomes to pay the mortgage or rent or put food on the table.

In your case, your wife says she wants to work – it's part of who she is – and that's also an important consideration. It's understandable that she might not want to put her career on hold, if that would mean she might miss out on opportunities for promotion or find it difficult to get the same kind of job when the children are a bit older. Isn't it healthy for the pair of you to sit down and discuss what you want to achieve personally, what you want to accomplish as a family, and where you can compromise within reason?

At the end of the day, each family is unique, and what works for one family won't necessarily work for another. The important thing is to be happy with the decisions you make as a couple and a family. Weigh the pros and cons. If both of you are happy at work, look for ways you can compromise and be flexible so that individual needs are met.

If the main issue you are dealing with is time management, you don't have that much to worry about. Spend some time drawing up a routine or schedule that takes into account all the key times during the day, and also draw up a timetable for the week that details all the other activities that regularly take place – shopping, after-school groups, and so on. Now, take a look at both timetables to see where the bottlenecks are. When both parents work, you can't wing it – you need good systems of organization and proper time management. For example, say Tuesday is football practice. Who picks up your son after the training session? Whose job is it to make sure he has his sports bag ready to take to school in the morning?

Here are some of the ways you can cope:

★ Get up earlier to allow more time for smooth hand-overs at school. Rotate the responsibility for getting the kids ready in the morning between the pair of you, and take turns at the end of the day to oversee the evening routine and put them to bed. Use these times to give your children some one-to-one attention.

★ If neither of you can leave work in time to pick up the children or ferry them around to different activities, put some support in place. Hire a part-time nanny, au pair, or babysitter to pick up the kids after school, or start a car pool with friends so you can share pick-ups and drop-offs.

★ Pin up a weekly timetable in the kitchen where you can keep track of appointments, school meetings, and all the other important details of family life. Make sure everyone knows who's responsible for what – including the kids – before you all leave the house in the morning.

★ Make sure you set aside enough time in the week to do things together as a family, to do things together as a couple, and for each of you to spend some time doing things for yourself. When working families feel the pressure, it's not the basics that generally suffer, it's the quality time. Leave your working life behind you when you leave the office and enjoy the time you spend together. Weekends should be about family.

★ Simplify your routine as much as possible. Don't overload your kids with lots of different activities to compensate for the time you spend at work. Let them focus on what they really enjoy doing. It may well be better for them to relax at home after school with a caregiver whom they like and trust than to be ferried from pillar to post.

★ Whenever possible, plan ahead so you aren't caught short by the unexpected. It's all about teamwork. Who's going to stay home if one of the kids is sick? Who's going to take time off work to watch your child perform in a school play or take part in a soccer match? However important your job is, these are milestones for your kids, and you need to make sure you are there for them.

Otherwise, if you feel your children are suffering in some way, or being short-changed, you are simply going to have to sit down with your wife and come to some kind of compromise. Bringing up your children is the most important responsibility and commitment either of you will ever have – parenting cannot be pushed to the edges and relegated to whatever time you have left over after the working day. Remember, looking after children is 24/7 – it's not overtime.

Take heart from the fact that many parents have tweaked their working lives to meet the demands of family life – perhaps taken an extra day at home during the week – and found that their careers have eventually taken off in new, satisfying, and rewarding directions.

Positive communication

A lot of parenting is about skillful communication. After all, kids aren't mind-readers. If you don't show them and tell them how you expect them to behave – in other words, lead by example – they won't know what's expected of them. If you say one thing and do another, they'll get mixed messages. If you get caught up in a whirlwind of emotion, lose control, and lash out at them verbally, you'll lower their self-esteem and breed a hostile relationship, which will only get worse.

The first thing parents need to do is to learn how to communicate with each other. Once you and your partner are on the Same Page (see below and page 30) and present a united front, your kids will know where they stand with you both. Mixed messages make kids feel confused and uncertain, and give them the opportunity to play one parent against the other.

Many of the problems I see in my work on *Supernanny* are made worse by the fact that Mom and Dad don't share the same approach in a particular area or are using their kids as a tool in their own power struggles with one another. Sometimes the differences show up in terms of discipline: Mom lets the children get away with the kind of behavior that Dad finds unacceptable, simply because she's worn out having to deal with it day after day. Or it might be the other way around – Dad has more of a soft touch because he doesn't get to spend much time with the kids, and laying down the law is the last thing he feels like doing when he gets home from work. Sometimes parents disagree on the rules – are the kids allowed sweets between meals or not? Are they allowed to stay up past their bedtimes on weekends or not? I don't know. Only you two do. Whatever your decision, make it together, on common ground.

When parents are not in agreement, it's not just the kids who suffer. Any parent who is struggling to enforce basic rules of behavior will feel undermined if that effort is not acknowledged or supported by their partner. If those efforts are not working, and the kids are running riot, the door is open wide for ridicule and condemnation. Then the blame game starts. It's all too easy in such situations for one parent to start feeling like a failure, and for relationships to come apart at the seams. But think about it for a minute. Why are you competing with each other? You're both responsible for your family. You both need to make decisions and take responsibility for your actions.

If parents find themselves completely at sea when their kids act up day after day, the result will be a negative environment. Over and over again, I've had parents say to me: "We're not in charge, the kids are. They're controlling our lives." In these situations, it's not unusual for a parent's frustration to turn into anger – or despair. Then the family stops being a unit. Instead, it's just a group of unhappy people living under the same roof. The good news is that you can turn things around with a positive will to change and the determination to see it through.

Q My partner doesn't seem to understand how difficult I find it during the day looking after our son, who's three and a half, and our daughter, who's fifteen months. When we do manage to find the time to sit down and talk, we always end up fighting.

A A lot of my work is focused on getting parents to acknowledge that they're in the same boat and that they have to find positive ways of supporting each other and working together to bring up their kids. One of the ways I do this is with the **Same-Page Technique**.

If you and your partner are going to function as a team, you need to remind yourselves of what brought you together as a couple in the first place and *find some common ground*. When a family is under pressure, it's easy for resentments to build up on all sides. The Same-Page Technique will help you to stop blaming yourself and each other, and move on to a more positive approach together.

Find a quiet time to sit down with your partner. Each of you should have a pen and piece of paper. Then each of you should write down five strengths that the other has as a partner and as a parent. Now swap the lists over and read them out loud.

Focusing on what's positive is the first step in breaking the emotional log jam and getting you two communicating again. Recognize what each other does for the family and validate each other's needs and efforts so you both feel supported. From your letter, it's clear that the pair of you aren't communicating well and that you feel you aren't getting the right response from your husband. But he may feel unsupported, too. This technique is a good way of opening things up so you start to trust and encourage each other again.

Try it with your spouse and see what happens. Fighting is loss of emotional control. Being positive will allow you to move forward together. You can also use the Same-Page Technique to agree a on common approach so that your children know that there is one set of ground rules they have to follow.

I used the Same-Page Technique with one family who found it difficult to agree on the methods they used to discipline their kids, and who had fallen into the trap of undermining each other. Mom was emotionally empty and worn out, while Dad had been forced to assume all responsibility for discipline and frequently lost control of his temper. The pair of them argued constantly in front of the kids about their different approaches. I gave them each a box and asked them to write down their thoughts and the issues they wanted to resolve. Then I asked them to go to a room by themselves, exchange the boxes, and deal with the issues one by one. That way, they were able to discuss the rules in a calm and neutral space and come to some kind of compromise that could get them working as a team again.

Q My husband is much softer on our nine-year-old twins than I am. I use the Time-Out Room when they behave badly and it works – most of the time. The trouble is that if they act up in the evening, when he's home from work, he won't discipline them. If I try to use the Time-Out Room when he's home, he undermines me and lets the kids off the hook. He says he has so little time to spend with them, he doesn't want to be a "heavy" dad or they might hate him.

A If your kids were younger, you wouldn't be having any success with the Time-Out Room at all. When parents differ in their approaches to discipline or what the rules should be, it's very difficult to get children to behave properly. Because your twins are nine, they're able to separate their parents into compartments and accept that Dad has a softer touch than you.

You and your husband need to work out a shared approach. What I understand from what you say is that he feels guilty for not spending more time with the twins and is disempowering you so he can be the "good cop." He should appreciate that all children need boundaries, and one of the ways in which you set those boundaries in place is by using firm and fair control – techniques like the Time-Out Room. Without discipline, children quickly lose respect for their parents' authority. In a lot of families that I see, there's plenty of love, but not much respect. Your husband needs to know that discipline will not make your kids love him any less.

The very last thing you need to do in this situation is to air your differences in front of your children. They already know you don't agree about discipline, and if you argue it out in front of them, this will give them the perfect excuse to play the pair of you against each other, if they're not doing so already. Show unity.

Try the **One-in-Three Technique**. I use this for couples who keep going over and over the same issue without managing to resolve it, or who constantly power struggle with one another. Not moving on builds resentment. Forgiving is one of the hardest things to do, but once you forgive each other, you will move on from strength to strength.

Pick a time when you can be alone – when the kids are in bed or out, for example. Sit down together to discuss your differences over discipline and allow yourselves a set time to resolve them. For this technique, I use a kitchen timer to set a time limit. This helps couples to concentrate and really focus on the issue at hand, and not drag a hundred and one other things into the discussion to throw at each other as ammo.

Discuss your differences calmly and rationally, and see if you can find a resolution. Nothing can be resolved when two people are angry. Try to find out why he is undermining you. Does he know that he is? If he is still reluctant to use the Time Out, see if you can work out a compromise so that at least you can keep going with the technique yourself. Don't let it be interrupted.

Q I've been trying to use the Naughty Step to discipline our two kids, who are four and six. The trouble is that when they misbehave when my husband is home, he slaps them. Now the kids won't take the Naughty Step seriously. What do I do? I don't believe in physical punishment, but my husband says he was spanked as a boy and it never did him any harm.

A Where physical contact is used as a reprimand, it will always outweigh any other technique because a child is going to be fearful. In these circumstances, alternative techniques will always be undermined. In homes where the Naughty Step and similar techniques are the methods of control, they are very effective.

In one family I knew, Dad would use harsher punishment. When I introduced the Naughty Chair as a means of disciplining their little boy, the child couldn't take it seriously. It was an uphill struggle at first to get him to respond to the technique. At one point, after repeated bad behavior, I asked his mother to take the boy's video game away as well for two days – and this really hit home. It was a far better punishment for the behavior the little boy had been displaying.

I had a similar situation with a family called the Youngs. For five unruly boys under the age of nine who were constantly getting into trouble, being asked to sit in a Naughty Chair was a joke. But this, in combination with other techniques, eventually began to turn their behavior around.

Physical punishment is not a form of discipline that allows a child to learn and progress.

What I would also say to you and your husband is that many parents, whether they realize it or not, fall back on the child-rearing methods that their own parents used, or they adopt a very similar style of parenting. This isn't surprising: It's what they know. But it doesn't have to be this way. As parents, you are shaping a future generation. Just because you were raised in a certain way doesn't mean you have to do the same by your kids. Society is changing all the time, and not necessarily for the worse. You have the chance to break that mold and bring up your children according to what you believe, not simply because it was the way you were raised. Step outside the box and make that difference now.

Of course, it can work both ways. Sometimes when parents feel that they were disciplined unfairly and too harshly when they were children, they become reluctant to set any boundaries at all for their kids. This is just as wrong. Kids need rules, boundaries, and discipline. But there are lots of effective ways you can teach your kids what the limits are without resorting to harsh punishment.

Q *How can I encourage my husband to help more around the home? I work three mornings a week, but the rest of the time I'm responsible for our three children, who are seven, five, and three, as well as all the housework. My husband says that his job is stressful and he needs the evenings to relax, but I get tired, too!*

A In families like yours where Dad goes out to work and Mom stays at home all or most of the time, it's obvious who's going to be doing the lion's share of the work in the house. Even so, it's important that both parents spend time with their kids, giving them individual attention.

Bringing up small children takes time, patience, and perseverance. It can be tiring without support – as you know. Moms who are coping on their own all day can struggle to manage the situation. Then Dad comes home in the evening to a stressed-out wife who may be full of resentment at the load she's been forced to carry without support. In some cases, Dad will respond by withdrawing almost completely from family life and responsibilities. I've seen Dads who managed to be "absent" even when they were still in the same room! It sounds like this might be going on in your case.

When I worked with the Gorbea family, it was obvious that Dad was taking a backseat in family life. As soon as I pointed that out to him, he admitted with a laugh that he'd finally been "caught out." He knew full well that he hadn't taken a very active role, and was quite happy to get stuck into the new routine and share the load.

In the Harmony family, Mom did everything and wouldn't allow Dad to help very often. They had three boys. The three-year-old, Grant, threw terrible tantrums where he would make noises like a Tyrannosaurus Rex and bite chunks out of the leather sofa as if he was a dinosaur feeding on it! Mom sometimes picked on Dad, with the consequence that he found it hard to address the out-of-control behavior, so Mom had to step in to deal with it herself, although her techniques were not working that well.

One of the first things I did for that family was to show them the **Trading-Tasks Technique**. I gave each parent a tray and loaded up the trays with weighted packets such as bags of sugar, each labeled with a different household task. As you might expect, Mom's tray was piled high, and there wasn't much on Dad's. Then I asked them both to carry their trays like waiters, supporting them only with the palm of one hand. The weight on Mom's tray was too much and she dropped it. I then gave her tray to her husband and asked him to imagine carrying that weight all day long on his back like a rucksack, how it would make his shoulders ache, how he would ache emotionally. This visual exercise helped both parents see how they should start sharing the load more fairly.

But many Moms really seem to enjoy wearing the martyr's crown. They will rush around doing everything to the point of exhaustion and resent every last minute. If they communicate their needs to their partners, it will take the form of criticism and blame. "I do everything! Can't you help me out once in a while?" Does this sound like you?

If so, pointing the finger is not the way to share the responsibilities of being a parent. You need to find a more effective approach.

Here are some ideas:

✶ Try the Same-Page Technique (page 30) to open up lines of communication in a positive way and agree upon a common approach.

✶ Another technique you can try is **Step Up/Step Back**. I used this technique when I was working with the Cantoni family, where Dad had been leaving most of the parenting responsibility to Mom. We drew up a poster to put on the wall. It had three boxes outlined on it. In the middle box, both parents were encouraged to list those areas they needed to work on so they could present a united front to their kids. Then Mom wrote down in her box those areas she needed to step back from. And Dad wrote in his box where he had to step up and take responsibility. It was a simple visual aid, but it helped both parents discuss ways they could improve their parenting styles together without blaming each other.

✶ Set up a routine so that you take turns to look after the kids during the evening. Dads who spend all day at work can have quality time with the children while supervising their baths or reading a bedtime story – it doesn't have to involve rambunctious play.

✶ Share the chores! It's the twenty-first century, for heaven's sake. You don't need to be knocking yourself out doing all the housework. Or cut back expenses in one area and hire a housekeeper.

✶ Do more things together as a family, not just the chores. Playing games together or going on outings can build a sense of togetherness that will encourage you and your husband to work together.

✶ Get the support you need. For you, it might be Time-Out during the week so you can look after yourself and recharge your batteries. Make some time for yourselves as a couple, too, so you can both step out of the parenting shoes for a little while.

✶ Just because your husband is at work all day doesn't mean he can't pick up the phone and offer a little support or ask how things are going. Don't spend the conversation recounting everything that's gone wrong or trying to make him feel guilty. Exchange information or just have a chat. An adult voice to talk to can make a huge difference if you're at home looking after small children and you feel isolated. Some of the families I've worked with in the States live miles from the nearest town, and Moms can go all day without much interaction with the outside world. Adult human contact, even by phone, can make all the difference.

In the Young family, both parents worked shifts and never had time to talk. Time was so tight that Mom and Dad had to exchange cars and the kids in a parking lot just to get to work on time. I gave each of them a tape recorder so they could record a running commentary on the day and keep each other up to speed. Then when Mom and Dad exchanged cars, the parent who was in charge of the kids could listen to the tape on the way home. The kids recorded their own messages, too, and playback always made them laugh. It was an aid to better insight and showed the parents that they had to make the time, however limited, to talk to each other at handover points so they could be consistent in their parenting.

Tip: Say it with flowers

I've worked in families where husbands left notes for their wives or sent flowers to show their appreciation for the way they were holding down the home and the family. There was a limit to what those fathers could do during the day when they were at work or away on a business trip, but the acknowledgment of the effort that their partners were making made all the difference to the way the pair related as couples and as parents.

Q *My wife and I have one son, Sam, who's three and a half, and we're expecting another baby in a couple of months' time. My wife gets pretty tired these days and I'd like to help her out more than I do, but Sam always insists on having Mommy do everything. I've tried to explain to him that he will have a little brother or sister soon and he can't expect to have Mommy to himself all the time, but he throws a tantrum every time I try to step in and help put him to bed or get him dressed in the morning. To be honest, I'm beginning to feel like a spare part in this family, and I'm worried things are only going to get worse when the baby comes along.*

A I really feel for you. It's not pleasant to feel sidelined, or powerless to perform your role as a parent. But you've got one important thing going for you, and that's the fact that you really want to be a committed Dad to your son. Some fathers have been faced with a similar situation, and as a result have retreated, shrugged their shoulders, and taken a backseat in family life, and then regretted they have done so.

It doesn't have to be that way. Your son needs both his parents, and your wife needs all the rest she can get, now and for some months to come. You've got a window of opportunity here to change the dynamic so that things are running more smoothly once the new baby arrives.

Mom must step back and allow you to fulfill your role. If you don't know how to cope with your son's behavior, she should show you how so you can gain confidence in your parenting. Telling Sam he can't expect to have Mommy to himself all the time sends out a discouraging message that he's too young to really understand.

So what should you do? First, you have to recognize why Sam is behaving the way he is. He's using his refusal to be looked after by anyone else but Mom as a means of control. So the first thing you both need to do is to break that pattern. That means you have to come up with a rotation and stick to it. One night, Mom puts Sam to bed; the next night you do. When it's your night, explain to Sam that you will be putting him to bed tonight and that it will be Mommy's turn tomorrow. At first, your son is going to try all his usual tricks to get Mom to come to the rescue. Your wife will need to be very firm and stay out of the picture so you get the chance to follow through. If you can see a tantrum coming, keep calm and nip it in the bud before it gets a chance to escalate. Try the Separation Technique (page 119).

I once visited a family on *Supernanny* where the dynamic was similar to yours, but the other way around. The Douglases had twins of four: a boy and a girl. Sandra's relationship with her daughter, Nicole, was very difficult, and at times she felt so rejected by Nicole that she had fantasized about leaving the family. The situation was made worse by the fact that every time Sandra had a problem dealing with her daughter – whether it was in the car, or in the bath – Douglas, the dad, would ride to the rescue and take over. Sandra had to learn to stay firm and not give in to Nicole's tantrums. Just as important, Dad needed to learn how to stay out of the picture so that

Mom and daughter had a chance to build their relationship.

In that situation, there was an underlying reason why Sandra let Nicole walk all over her. When the twins were very young, Sandra was called away on a serious emergency having to do with her work for an airline. While she was gone, Doug built up a bond with the twins and coped really well. When she returned, Sandra felt guilty that she had left the twins at such a young age, and Doug was worried he would lose his special connection with them when Mom returned.

But being a parent isn't just about sharing the load with your partner. It's also about having quality time with your kids. Play a game with your son – just the two of you – or find some activity, such as kicking a ball around in the park, which can be a special time for you both. Go out as a family and have some fun together so that Sam learns he can have a good time without demanding all of Mom's attention for himself.

He's already shown how he feels about sharing Mom's attention with you. Sharing it with a baby is going to be very challenging for him.

For that reason, you need to prepare him for the new arrival much better than you're doing at the moment. Choose your words carefully. If you tell him that he's going to have less of Mom's attention once the baby comes, he's going to really dread that day. Every time a parent talks to a child, that child is going to wonder: "What does that mean?" Kids take things very literally. How much of what you say is backed up by the way you behave? Are you sending out mixed messages to him? Don't use the new baby as a threat. Instead, bolster your son's confidence and independence by using the Involvement Technique (page 157) to teach him how to help and cooperate. Tell him he's going to be a big brother soon. (See page 156 for more ways to prepare a child for the birth of a sibling.)

C is for Confidence.
Make your decisions confidently and show your kids you're happy in your role. It's all in the tone of voice and body language.

Q *I'm a thirty-six-year-old mother of two children. Jason is eight and Chloe is ten. They never listen to a word I say. I find myself telling them to do things over and over until I'm sick of the sound of my voice. Chloe is the worst – if I take her to task over the smallest thing, we end up having a screaming match. How am I going to cope when they're older? I find it really upsetting because they do everything their Dad tells them to. What am I doing wrong?*

A Yelling, nagging, screaming, losing it – these aren't good ways of communicating with children. But you already know that because when you nag, yell, or shout, all you communicate to your children is that you have lost control. Once they've picked that up, they will lose respect for you, and you won't be any closer to getting them to behave or do what they're told. A child's behavior will get progressively worse when it feeds off a loss of control.

I'm constantly amazed at the kinds of things parents say to their kids:
"Do you know how bad you make me feel?"
"Go away and leave me alone!"
"You're such a mess-up! You're so ******
annoying!"
"Shut up when I'm talking to you!"
"Get out of here! Go to your room and stay there!"

If you want to tear a strip off your child, if you want to make her feel small and destroy her self-esteem, you're going about it in the right way. Some parents pride themselves that they would never raise a hand to their kids, but have no hesitation in wounding them with vicious words. It's abuse, plain and simple.

So how should you talk to your children? With respect. With love. With clarity. With understanding. With calmness.

How should you talk to your children when they're upset or in need of understanding, or when emotions are raw? Listen to what they have to say. Don't interrupt them, shut them out, or brush them aside. Validate their feelings and give them guidance without jumping to conclusions or giving them a pat answer. Sometimes you may find yourself in a situation where your child has a problem that is beyond your power to solve there and then. Parents often respond to such issues by revealing their panic, frustration, or anxiety. Stay calm. Say to your child: "How are we going to deal with this?" Give her the guidance to encourage her to think for herself. Show her that you have a grasp of the bigger picture, even if a solution doesn't immediately present itself. How you respond will play a big part in how your child deals with the issue.

That's *how* you should talk to your children. The tone of voice you should use is a different story altogether. I always say that parents need at least three different tones of voice:

★ The **EVERYDAY VOICE** is an even tone that you should use in conversation with your children. If you bark out commands at your kids or order them around in a harsh, loud tone, you immediately communicate the fact that you expect them not to do as they're told. If you sound stressed and at the end of your tether, the same is true. Be polite when you are asking your children to do something. You can't expect your children to have good manners if you aren't polite to them. "Please wash your hands and come to the table." "Could you tidy up your room, please?" Keep your voice even and reasonable, not apologetic, or even pleading.

★ If your child has done something wrong or has not done as you asked, you need to use the **VOICE OF AUTHORITY**. Don't shout from halfway across the room or rip into her. Go to her, get down to her level, and make direct eye contact. If she tries to look away or move away, hold her arms and say: "Look at me, please. I am talking to you." Use a low, firm, authoritative tone to tell her what she has done wrong. "I asked you to tidy up your room. I want you to do it now, please." Ignore any attempts by your child to talk back, argue, or bargain. Separate the behavior from the child: You are not damning her, you are making it clear that the behavior is unacceptable to you.

★ If your child still refuses to do what she's been told, you should give her a warning, using the Voice of Authority, that she will be disciplined if she does not comply. (See the Naughty Step and beyond, page 168, for the type of techniques you can use.) It is important to give just ONE warning, and then take action. Three, four, five, six warnings and your child will realize that all you are issuing are empty threats.

★ The third type of voice is the **VOICE OF APPROVAL**. It's a high, excited voice that communicates pleasure. Use it to praise your child for good behavior – especially when she's done something right without being asked to. "Thank you for clearing the table. Well done!" Be careful with older children not to patronize them. If all you do is pull your children up short whenever they have done something wrong, but never praise them when they've been good, your kids will come to see misbehaving as the only way to get your attention and receive unhealthy love.

A lot of people don't find it easy to express their authority calmly. Why not? Because they've already lost control. Some parents have to lose their temper before they feel able to express authority or find the courage to express themselves. Observe your children's behavior and identify what brings out a hostile reaction in you. Rather than blow your top, learn to respond to the behavior in a calm, direct, and authoritative way.

When parents find it difficult to assert themselves, I often get them to practice in front of a mirror until they are comfortable taking on the role. In the Collins family, for example, Mom was not very confident and was overwhelmed by the aggressive behavior of her kids. She was even embarrassed in front of the mirror, and shied away from looking at herself directly. (I called it the Lady Di look! You know the one – peering up from under her hair.) I explained to her that she needed to be able to take herself seriously before her kids would respect her.

Finally, think about why your daughter pushes your buttons more than your son.

In one of the families I've worked with, the Cookes, the relationship between the mother, Denise, and the oldest girl, Meghann, had become very difficult. Nine-year-old Meghann had a very strong character and could be very obstinate. Dealing with her behavior – rudeness, biting, hitting – had ground Denise down to the extent that she had no energy and felt inadequate on every level. Feeling like that meant that Denise felt too powerless to discipline her daughter, which, in turn, only made Meghann more confrontational. Denise was taking the punishment like a punching bag and when the two of them argued, it was like they were both fighting to have the last word. What was very revealing was that when they had a screaming match, Meghann was using exactly the same tone of voice as her mother. "No, actually, it was like this!" "It wasn't like this, actually, it was like that!" They were each fueling each other's fire.

It took time for Denise to see that she had to set the example, not stoop to Meghann's level. If you change, people have to change around you. And change was something that Meghann was threatened by. When Denise learned how to discipline her daughter without losing it, Meghann began to learn to take the consequences of her behavior and be accountable for it.

C is for Communication.
Keep talking and listening to your kids and to each other. It's the key to everything.

Q We have two children, Immie, who is coming up on eighteen months, and Aaron, who's nearly five. Aaron's behavior has never been very good. He's aggressive toward his sister, and he's a really fussy eater, no matter how much we try to encourage him and offer different foods. Yesterday he had a screaming fit at the table and made himself sick. When Aaron was two, he nearly died of meningitis, and sometimes we still can't believe how lucky we are to have him with us today, but his behavior is really getting to us. We've had him checked over by our doctor, who has assured us that there's no physical reason for it.

A Traumatic events such as Aaron's illness are a shock to the system, and take a lot of getting over. Watching a child fight for his life is any parent's worst nightmare. Luckily, as you say, your family came through this terrible event and your son recovered. I'm sure you count your blessings every day.

Aaron's present behavior is nothing that could not be addressed with proper boundaries and firm control. Use the Naughty-Step Technique (or one of its variations, see page 172) to teach him not to be aggressive to his sister.

Don't offer him too much choice at mealtimes. Put a small portion of what everyone else is eating down in front of him. If he doesn't eat, tell him he can leave the table when he has had three (or four, or five) mouthfuls. Encourage! Don't allow him to snack to make up for what he doesn't eat at

the table. When he starts to become disruptive, make it clear that the behavior is unacceptable and remove him to the Naughty Step before he has a chance to throw a screaming fit and make himself sick.

In many ways, Aaron is behaving like a toddler. That tells me one thing, which is that you and your partner are still where you were mentally and emotionally when your son was very sick. And because you're living in the past, you are not able to let Aaron progress and teach him how to be more mature in his behavior. Your doctor has given him a clean bill of health. You need to move on and become more confident and less anxious as parents.

Learn from your past experience, let it go, and move on.

I saw something very similar in the Tsironis family. In that case, twin three-year-old boys were out of control and demanding all the attention of both parents, while their sister, who was four, missed out on attention. The twins had been born very premature at twenty-three weeks' gestation, weighing little more than a pound each. It was a miracle that they pulled through. The parents had to learn to let go of the trauma of the boys' birth and put some discipline in place to get their family back on track. When they started to implement the Naughty-Point Technique (page 182), they were freed from the constant struggle for control. At the same time, they were able to communicate better as a couple and look forward to the future, rather than dwell on the past.

In another family, the Mom had difficulty interacting with her youngest child. His behavior was challenging, to say the least — he regularly spat, hit and bit. It emerged, after discussing things over with the couple, that Mom was carrying a lot of guilt. Her youngest's birth had not gone according to plan, and had eventually resulted in an emergency Caesarean. Ever since, she could not shrug off the sense that it was all her fault. Once this was brought out in the open, and she was encouraged to see that she had nothing to blame herself for, she was able to build a better relationship with her son.

Carrying baggage from the past can prevent you from enjoying your children now, teaching them what they need to know, and making life-changing decisions that are positive. If you don't release negative feelings, they work like an energy block. Learn to let go and move on, and you won't look back!

Family patterns

Families come in all shapes and sizes these days. The extended family, with several generations living close by each other, may be a thing of the past in many cultures and societies, but new patterns have come to take its place. Step-families, where children share their time between two homes; single-parent families; and families where both parents work are all on the increase. With developments in fertility treatment, fostering, and adoption, older parents are also becoming more common.

Whatever form your family takes, it is important not to feel that you are letting your kids down in any way because your family doesn't conform to a so-called perfect stereotype. What is that, anyway? There's no such thing as perfect. All families have strengths and weaknesses, whatever pattern they take. Learn to play up your strengths, work on the trouble spots, and rest assured that you are doing your best by your kids. Accept that your family is unique and very special.

Q Ever since my partner walked out three years ago, I've been raising my two kids (Lisa, aged four, and Ryan, aged nine) on my own. The children's father has moved to another country and has broken off contact. He sends a little money from time to time, but as it's not enough for us to live on, I had to go back to work to keep a roof over our heads. I'm tired all the time and often find myself snapping at the kids for no good reason. Ryan's been getting into trouble at school, and Lisa is very clingy. I don't want to fail my kids because of the situation we find ourselves in, but I just don't know what to do to make things better. I know that some of the other mothers at school think Ryan's a handful because he hasn't got a dad, and this makes me feel terrible.

A First of all, I have a lot of respect and admiration for the way you are trying to deal with the demands of bringing up your kids by yourself. Single parents have a tough time. If it isn't the press wading in, blaming single Moms for each and every one of society's ills (yet single Dads are given admiration), it's the widespread view that children from single-parent households are going to miss out in their family dynamic. Unfortunately, the divorce rate is very high. But there are many successful single parents out there who are raising happy and well-adjusted children. Remind yourself that bringing up your kids in an atmosphere that isn't poisoned by conflict is much better than forcing them to grow up in an unhappy home with parents who simply cannot get along, with each other. What you can't change, you

have to accept. Your partner has broken off contact – that's a fact. What you have to do is put your energies into being solid and consistent for your kids, so your family can get back on track.

When relationships break up, it takes time for the dust to settle emotionally. You obviously found yourself dropped into the deep end straight away when you had to go back to work to support yourself and your kids after their father left. Have you had the opportunity to talk to anyone, or has it just been a struggle to cope? Feelings of sadness, failure, and anger are common when relationships come to an end. You may find it very helpful to share these with a friend, family member, or a group of single parents who are going through similar experiences – or even a counselor. Negative feelings make parents less confident when they are handling their children; lack of confidence leads, in turn, to loss of control, and then it's easy to feel overwhelmed. Feeling bad about yourself or your situation is also draining – it might be part of the reason why you are so tired.

Of course, break-ups have an impact on children, too. Your daughter would have been too young at the time of the split to remember her father, but she will be aware of how much you are struggling. Your son may be experiencing some of the same feelings as you, and often that does manifest itself in school behavior problems. Have you tried to talk to him about it? It's important to reassure him that you will be there for him. When one parent has walked out – and, worse, broken off contact – a child loses a certain degree of trust in the world. He'll need to build up his confidence again. Talk to his school and let them know; everyone needs to show compassion.

What your children need more than ever are clear rules and boundaries, backed up by firm control when necessary. They need to know where they stand, and while their behavior is understandable, you have to work to change it. Give them both some small responsibilities – tidying up, for example, or setting the table. Your son is old enough to help you in many ways, and your daughter will gain confidence if you give her small, achievable tasks to do. Get them involved, and you will start to function in your new shape as a family again.

What is very important is that you aren't tempted to treat your children as friends or equals. They need you to be their parent, their Mom, someone who sets them an example and makes sure that they keep to the rules. And that's why it's also very important to find an adult with whom you can share your troubles and concerns. If you share your worries with your children, you are burdening them with a role they are not equipped to handle. Kids who find themselves in the position of caring for their own parent often experience difficulties later in life simply because they were forced into an adult role when they had no resources to deal with it.

You don't have to put up with the cards you've been dealt and struggle on with no assistance. Get involved with local or church groups and put some support systems in place – ask your friends and family for help. Spend some time in the week doing something just for you. Put something back in the bank, and you'll find yourself less likely to snap at your children because you are feeling stressed and overwhelmed.

Finally, make time for things you can do together as a family. Play a game with your kids after work – the chores can wait. Take your kids on outings – if you're on a budget, a trip to the park costs nothing. Whatever you can do together will reinforce your new family unit and make it stronger. Don't look at your family as a chair with the leg missing. A three-legged stool is just as good!

D is for Determination.

Focus on achieving your positive goals and make sure you follow through. Find your inner strength!

Q *My problem is my daughter Sue. She's had a tough time – she's a single mom – and in the last few months she's just got back on her feet and started a new part-time job. After she split up with her partner, she was very low for a while and I offered to take the kids off her hands for a few afternoons a week to give her a bit of a break. But now that Sue's working again and things are getting back on an even keel, I've tried to suggest that she could make other arrangements – there's a good nursery school nearby that the kids could go to, and she earns enough now to afford a babysitter to pick them up and look after them until she gets home. She says that she doesn't want to do this, and that there isn't anyone else that she'd trust to look after the kids.*

Don't get me wrong – I love my grandkids to bits – and we have great times. But they really wear me out! Clare is four, and what we would have called "a right little madam" in my day, and Jack is two and a half, and into everything. I feel I've done my stint as a mother, and when I see my friends who are enjoying being grandparents without the stresses and strains, I feel like I'm missing something. Am I being unfair?

A Not at all! What a fortunate woman your daughter is to have your love and support when she was at such a low ebb. We all know that families aren't as tight-knit as in years gone by, but this is a wonderful example of how strong and supportive family ties can be.

But Sue's on her own two feet now, and you have every right to want your role as a grandparent back. Sit down with your daughter and explain how you feel over a cup of tea. Tell her that you recognize that she's in a different place, and that you are proud of the way she has picked up the pieces of her life. Say that you would like to go back to your role as the kids' granny now; that you will still look after the kids from time to time, but you want to be able to enjoy them as a grandparent, too. It's good to be honest about your feelings. You may find that she is more than willing to see things from your perspective.

Sue has leaned on you in her time of need, and she's obviously very comfortable with the present arrangement. But it will be healthy for her to let other people into her life to care for her kids. You can still give her support in other ways – by helping her choose a sitter, for example, or by offering to babysit on Saturday nights. The role of grandparents is so important. You have time, patience, and tons of love to offer your grandkids, all the more so if you are not acting as co-care giver.

I've come across this type of issue a few times on *Supernanny*. Debbie Senior lived next door to her parents, and had come to rely on them to discipline her kids and play with them – a situation not helped by the fact that the fence was down between the two properties and the kids were free to run over to their grandparents whenever they felt like it. I had to encourage Debbie to become more confident and take up her parenting duties. I literally put the boundaries back in place, by getting the fence rebuilt and putting a lock on the gate, so that when the kids found it locked, they knew that their grandparents didn't want to be disturbed.

Q *After years of trying and several courses of IVF, my wife and I found ourselves the proud parents of triplets – the girls are now nearly three. We thought we knew what we were in for, but nothing could have prepared us for the way our lives have been turned upside down. Although we managed the first year pretty well (I took some leave from work so there was another pair of hands at home), as the girls have grown older, it's got progressively harder for my wife. Some days it's all she can do to get them dressed and fed. My wife is forty-three and I'm forty-seven, so we're a little old to be first-time parents. Can you give us a few pointers on how to cope?*

A First of all, congratulations! As I'm sure you know already, it's a big enough challenge looking after a new baby in the early months – triplets multiply that challenge three times and more. All parents of twins and triplets say the first nine months are incredibly hard work. I'm so impressed that you supported each other through that difficult and exhausting time. And well done for taking leave from your work and putting your family first – that was the right thing to do. It sounds like you and your wife work really well together and support each other, which is brilliant.

Twins and triplets are more common in older parents (over the age of thirty-five, a woman's chance of conceiving twins is much higher). Multiple births are also much more common when you have fertility treatment, as I am sure you were told. But, as you say, nothing quite prepares you for the reality of feeding, changing, and soothing three babies

at the same time. How could it? But it's three times the joy.

One of the families I visited on *Supernanny*, the Burnetts, had two sets of twins under three. If ever a Dad needed to be an octopus, it was Michael, who looked after all four of them during the day while his wife was at work – while trying to run his business from home at the same time. I'm going to suggest to you what I told the Burnetts, and that is to work out a timetable. Sit down with your wife and plan out a daily routine. Put a framework into place so that you and your wife aren't just reacting to events; you have a structure to work to. Break the day down into half-hour periods, starting with key points, such as mealtimes, and go on to fill in the details, with scheduled times for different kinds of play. (For more on how to create a routine, see page 15.) Focus on the trouble spots, and see if you can work out a way to share the load. If you need to get off to work by a set time in the morning, for example, make sure the girls get up early enough so that you can give your wife a hand.

Whether you have twins or triplets, there simply aren't enough hours in the day to stagger their care, so you will need to feed, dress, and bathe the girls all together at the same time. You've only got twenty-four hours to work with, so create a routine for them so you can sleep yourself. One of the ways in which parents of twins or triplets come unstuck is by attending to each child in turn – that's how it can take all day just to get everyone dressed and fed. And when all day is given over to basic care, your children won't be getting the stimulation and attention they need from play and new experiences, which means they are more likely to get bored and misbehave. A routine will allow you and your wife the time to attend to each child's individual personality and character.

If you and your wife are finding it harder now that the girls are older, why is that? Perhaps you found it easier to deal with their physical needs when they were tiny, but lack the techniques to deal with the way they are developing now. If you are still relating to them as if they were babies, you may well be making matters worse. They may be triplets, but they're three-year-old toddlers first and foremost. This is an age when kids like to test the limits and see how far they can go. Your triplets are at the exploring stage.

There are two main things you can do to ease the situation. First, set some clear boundaries for your triplets so they know what the rules are, and back these up using one of the techniques described in the chapter The Naughty Step and Beyond (page 168). Second, encourage your girls to be more independent by giving them small achievable tasks to do. A three-year-old should be able to dress herself with a little help and to feed herself, even if she does it messily. She can even be invited to "help" in simple ways – ask her to fetch something for you or put something away. Give your girls plenty of praise each time they do something for themselves. "Good girl, you found your shoes! Now put them on, please. Shall Daddy show you how?" As your girls learn to be more self-sufficient, they will feel a real sense of pride in what they are learning.

Other useful tips for coping with twins or triplets:

★ It's very tempting to dress your kids in identical clothes – it looks so cute, and when you're out with them it always gets a response from other people. But each child needs to gain the sense of who they are individually – not simply as a twin or triplet. Allow them to develop their own personalities and learn to see them as separate people in their own right. Dressing them in different clothes is an important first step: Let them decide and help choose what to wear.

★ If one child is acting up when you are playing a game, discipline that child, but not the other two. Keep on with the game and make it clear to the child who misbehaved that after the period of discipline is over and you have had an apology, she can join in again. Teach the Shared-Play Technique (page 219).

★ Twins and triplets are special. They're a lovely dynamic to watch in action. How amazing it must be to grow alongside another person or persons, right from the womb. You'll often find that they'll play together easily, complement each other, and support each other's strengths and weaknesses.

★ Don't be afraid to ask for help. Contact a triplets or multiple-birth support group. Get a friend, family member, or mother's helper in for a few hours a week to ease the burden.

Finally, older parents are not better or worse than parents who had their kids in their twenties or early thirties. Recognize your strengths and play to them. You may well have greater reserves of patience than younger parents, even if your energy levels aren't so high. Remember that, whatever your age, you're never too old to find your inner child. Let down your hair and have fun with your kids! Do what is necessary for *you* so that *you* become self-confident.

2 Mealtimes

Mealtimes are one of the cornerstones of your daily routine. When you have small children, it's very important that you are consistent in this respect and that they sit down to eat at roughly the same times every day. It's also important that those times are spaced far enough apart so that your kids have an appetite for what's put in front of them, but not so far apart that the prelude to every meal is marked by the kind of bad behavior and irritability that's triggered by hunger and low blood sugar levels.

But meals are not just about getting the right amount and type of food into your kids at the right time. They're also occasions when families should be together, sharing news, talking over what everyone's been up to during the day, and enjoying each other's company. European countries, where children are welcome at the table, have always led the way in this respect.

In many families, mealtimes aren't like that. Instead, they're running battles – battles to get kids to eat, battles to get kids to behave, battles to get kids to sit down at the table at all. When you're dealing with these kinds of issues, a mealtime isn't relaxing, it's a war zone.

I'm constantly amazed at the sort of diet many parents offer their kids and expect them to thrive on. Junk food; frozen meals; fizzy drinks high in sugar, salt, and caffeine; snacks, snacks, and more snacks – in some homes, kids are grazing all day. Some parents excuse this by saying it's all their kids will eat – but no child was born craving a poor diet high in salt, fats, and sugar. If that's all he's offered, a child *learns* to prefer

these foods. I've heard parents say: "I just don't know why they eat so much junk!" Hello? Who goes shopping? Who puts the food in the cupboards and the fridge? Some parents shut their kids up by offering them these kinds of foods, creating a link between food and emotions that is very unhealthy. We've got record levels of childhood obesity, childhood diabetes, and eating disorders. Parents need to be more savvy about what they give their kids to eat.

Every child needs a healthy nutritional diet right from the get-go. Food provides the fuel for physical and mental activity. It nourishes your child's body, so that it grows and develops. The right diet also has a huge impact on a child's concentration and behavior, so he is better equipped mentally to learn. We're learning more every day about the impact certain foods have on the way our bodies function, from foods that bolster our immune system to those that improve memory and concentration. When Jamie Oliver launched his campaign to improve school meals in Britain, the impact of food on behavior was very clear. Once he had got the fast food off the menu and encouraged cafeteria staff to start cooking nutritious meals again, discipline problems in those schools he was working with fell dramatically. He promoted healthy attitudes to food, made the message fun, and reached out to millions in a positive way.

One of the reasons why mealtimes are so stressful in many households is that feeding children can't help but be an emotional issue for parents. Some Moms and Dads worry that if their kids don't eat, they will wither away to nothing. Then, when kids pick up on the anxiety, eating starts becoming an issue of control, a form of emotional blackmail. Before long, you're hopping around cooking three different suppers for your three kids, most of which you know you're going to wind up throwing in the trash. In other families, problems with eating occur because kids are not exposed to enough variety of foods at an early age.

Let's get mealtimes back on track again. It's up to parents to set good examples for their kids so they learn healthy eating patterns. And it's also up to parents to put rules and boundaries in place so that the family meal stops being a free-for-all and becomes an enjoyable part of the day.

Nutritious food is only one part of a healthy lifestyle. Kids need to eat good food in the right quantity. But they also need plenty of physical activity in the open air to burn off excess energy. And they need a decent period of sleep every night so they are rested for the next day. Food, activity, sleep, mental stimulation: It's not complicated. These are the basics that we all need to function at our best.

Tip: Forward planning
If you are pressed for time during the day, prepare food in advance of mealtimes. Chop the vegetables, season the meat, and make the patties when you're not in constant demand, then chill them in the fridge until it's time to cook. Or you can cook a large batch of stew, soup, or pasta sauce and freeze individual portions so that you always have something on hand.

Topics and techniques covered in this chapter:

HOW TO EAT TOGETHER AS A FAMILY

THE TALKING-STICK TECHNIQUE to get families communicating over the dinner table

THE LITTLE-CHEF TECHNIQUE to get your kids involved with meal preparation

BREASTFEEDING guidelines and problem areas

WEANING – how to introduce solid food and which foods to feed

CHAOTIC MEALTIMES and what to do about them

THE GOOD-EATER TECHNIQUE for fussy eating and food phobias

THE PLACEMAT REWARD CHART for positive feedback

SNACKING do's and don'ts

THE SNACK-JAR TECHNIQUE to control snack times

E is for Effort.
You get what you put in. Go the extra mile in everything you do, and you will be rewarded with results.

How to eat together as a family

I think it's very important that families should try to eat together as much as possible. Eating is not just about refueling, it should be a sociable time when kids learn to interact well with each other and their parents. Statistics show that families are spending less and less time with each other, particularly at meals, and this is a very worrying trend.

Time after time, I see families where mealtimes are completely fragmented. Kids are allowed to snack all day or help themselves to what they want from the fridge or kitchen cupboards. Meals are taken in front of the TV, whenever, whatever. Parents never eat with their kids or even supervise their mealtimes. Yet the same parents often turn around and complain that they can't take their kids to a restaurant or to a meal at a friend's house because they behave so badly. How can kids learn to behave at the table if they're never there in the first place?

When children are very small, the last meal of the day needs to be pretty early by adult standards, between 4:30 and 5:30 p.m., so that there is plenty of time for the kids to wind down and get to bed at a reasonable hour. For most families, where one or both parents work, this tends to rule out shared family meals during the week. Weekends and holidays, however, are a different matter. Take advantage of time off to sit down with your kids and eat together, whenever it is.

While older kids can eat together without supervision, you shouldn't leave young ones to their own devices at mealtimes during the week – they need encouragement and help with their motor skills to enable them to learn coordination. Even if you plan to eat later with your partner, you can still sit down at the table with your kids and have a drink, a snack, or piece of fruit. Don't hover over them anxiously like a bossy head waiter, or disappear out of the room to get on with another chore. Take the time to sit at the table and encourage them to eat and behave well. Talk to your kids! And it's never too early to start teaching them basic manners. Even young children can be taught to say "Please" and "Thank you."

Establish some basic ground rules for mealtimes:

* Children should wash their hands before they eat.
* They should sit at the table and not run off and eat their food somewhere else.
* No meals in front of the TV. The TV stays off during meals.
* Children should stay at the table until you tell them that they can be excused (but be realistic about how long they can last).
* No food fighting or spitting.
* No yelling or screaming.
* "Please" and "Thank you" are important words to learn!

Sitting at the table is a learning experience for the whole family. As soon as your baby can sit upright without additional support, bring her highchair to the table. Let her feed herself as much as possible – with finger foods to start off. When she is big enough, give her a booster seat and her own place at the table. I've seen kids as old as two and a half or three still stuck in highchairs drinking from bottles or sippy cups. Let your kids try new challenges. You should encourage their growing independence. If they make a mess in the process, let them. It's how they learn. Put newspapers or plastic sheets down on the floor, wrap your kids up in bibs, but don't hinder their development.

Parents sometimes worry too much about table manners. Be realistic here. Set sensible ground rules and insist on basic politeness – please and thank you. By all means, teach your children not to leave the table with their mouths full.

Tip: Be the boss of the remote control

I've been in homes where the kids were glued to the TV all day. I've also been in homes where TVs were blaring in three separate rooms, not counting the video game on the computer. Too much TV! Parents, you've got to take the lead here. Decide how much TV your kids should watch and which programs are suitable for their ages and temperaments. Don't let them watch scary programs – keep an eye on how they react and be prepared to switch off the box if they are getting upset. Don't let kids play video games or watch action movies just before bedtime – it over-stimulates them.

The Youngs were an American family I visited. The little girl, Shelby, had her meals in front of the television while everyone else ate at the table. My first step was to turn the TV off and bring Shelby to the table with the rest of the family. Then I worked on getting the family to communicate with each other over dinner. I used a Talking Stick that I bought at a Native American reservation in the desert. In tribal discussions, the Talking Stick was traditionally used to allow everyone to have their say. The chief would hand it to another member of the tribe and that person could talk as long as he was holding the stick. Placing the stick beside the placemat of each person in the Young family got them used to listening to each other and taking turns to communicate. It was a great incentive for all the family.

F is for Family.
Recognize the uniqueness of your family and embrace it.

Tip: Happy meals

If your kids already have good healthy eating patterns, why not make mealtimes fun once in a while? Special plates, cups, napkins, and placemats that feature their favorite cartoon characters, squiggly straws in drinks, and food cut into funny shapes lighten up the occasion and give them something to look forward to. I've used cookie cutters and molds to stamp out potato dinosaurs and brown rice ducks . . . Use your imagination and give your kids a treat. Be adventurous with color and presentation. Food is more appetizing when it looks inviting.

Family meals aren't just about sitting down at the table to eat. Get your kids involved in the preparation. Make it a joint effort. This gives kids a real sense of achievement. They are less likely to disrupt a meal they have helped to produce. I call this the **Little-Chef Technique**.

HOW THE TECHNIQUE WORKS

★ Give each child her own task to accomplish. It may be fetching plates and setting the table, it may be writing out a menu, it may be stirring a cake mix or washing the vegetables. Make the tasks achievable and appropriate for the age of the child.

★ Give plenty of encouragement and praise for a job well done.

One of the families I visited, the Amarals, own and run their own restaurant. Pressure from work meant that both parents were finding it difficult to devote enough time to their kids. In the absence of positive attention, the boys were using the restaurant as an amusement park, tearing through the dining room and generally acting up, much to the despair of the other staff – and the astonishment of customers! I worked with the family to develop a routine that created a better balance between work and home life, and encouraged Mike, the dad, to spend an extra day away from the restaurant. I also used the Little-Chef Technique to get the boys involved in mealtime preparation. Mike's a chef, and he was thrilled to see how four-year-old Logan really enjoyed cooking alongside him. Nine-year-old Ryan had fun drawing up the menus, and even the toddler, Kade, joined in. The technique turned a chore into a happy family occasion where Dad could really bond with his boys. His passion in the kitchen rubbed off on them.

KEY POINT

Getting your kids involved in preparing meals doesn't mean letting them loose with sharp knives and pans of boiling water, or letting them get up onto the counter near a flaming burner. Use your common sense. By all means, teach them how to do new things, but make sure you supervise them at all times. Once they have mastered one task, you can move them onto something more challenging.

Tip: Kitchen safety
Be aware of the dangers in your kitchen. Keep your knives out of the reach of your kids. Turn pan handles away so that kids can't burn themselves. Keep bleaches and cleansers under lock and key.

Q I was determined to breastfeed our new baby daughter (our first child), but I'm finding it much harder than I thought. I just can't seem to get her to settle into a pattern. My breasts are very painful and sore, and my daughter cries all the time. I don't think she can be getting enough to eat. Please help. I don't want to give up and put her on the bottle – she's only six weeks – but I'm at the end of my tether!

A The first few weeks with a new baby is a special time, but there's no two ways about it – it's tiring, too. Are you getting what you need to function properly? Eating a healthy diet, drinking plenty of fluids, and resting as often as you can are all absolutely essential. Nap when she naps, get support from family and friends to help you with the shopping and cooking, and don't be too ambitious about what you take on the rest of the time. Take things as easy as you can.

Many new mothers are not given enough guidance on breastfeeding before they leave the hospital or the maternity ward. It doesn't always come naturally. If you have painful breasts and sore nipples, it's more than likely that your daughter is not latching on properly – and this can lead to mastitis, an infection in the milk ducts, which is very painful. Most of the brown area of the nipple (the aureole) should be in her mouth when she sucks. If she sucks just from the end of the nipple, she won't drain the breast properly. The milk ducts will become engorged and painful, and your nipples may dry out and crack. It is also important to offer each breast in turn so that each is properly drained. If she is full after she's had one side, offer the other the next time.

It is also important to understand that your breasts produce milk in response to your baby's demands. It's not unusual for feeding to take a bit of time to settle into a pattern or routine. Then, when it does, that pattern may change again a few weeks later and you may find your baby wants to nurse all the time. Don't despair. This doesn't mean that she is starving. It's just nature's way of increasing the amount of milk you produce to meet her growing needs. When you are producing more milk, the pattern will return.

Once you have managed to get her to latch on properly, she should take in more every time and become less fretful as a result. But don't always assume that crying means hunger – she may need burping or changing, for example.

Some babies take longer to find a pattern than others, but by about three to six weeks, most seem to settle into a routine of wanting to nurse every two to four hours. You can carry on nursing on demand, or you can adjust the pattern so that the intervals are easier for you to cope with. For example, by shifting feeding times slightly earlier each day, you may get to the point where you are woken less often at night.

If you find that you just can't make breastfeeding work and decide to put her on the bottle, don't beat yourself up about it.

Q *What age should I start to wean my baby? What kind of foods can I give her? She's three months now, and my mother says she's old enough to start on solids.*

A I would wait a while. Milk (breast milk or formula), along with cooled, boiled water, is all you should give your baby for the first four to six months. After that, you can begin to introduce new tastes into her diet. It's important not to rush things. A baby's digestive system takes time to develop to the point where it can cope with food other than milk. If you introduce solid food too early, it can lead to allergic reactions and stomach problems. When she starts to demand more and more milk, or if her weight gain has slowed for no reason, you'll know that it's the right time to try her on solids.

Start by offering her bland, semi-solid foods such as baby rice or baby cereal mixed with breast milk, formula milk, or cooled, boiled water. At the beginning, you are just offering tastes and textures. Don't expect her to take to it right away – it will be a whole new sensation for her. Set aside one mealtime to offer the new food. Breakfast or lunch is better than in the evening, when she'll be more tired. And make sure you keep on offering her plenty of water.

After a baby has gotten used to the cereal or baby rice, I start introducing cooked, puréed root vegetables. Then comes cooked, puréed fruit. Later on you can introduce protein such as cooked, puréed chicken – white meat first. Then move on to dark meat, like minced lamb or beef. Make sure all food is mashed or puréed so there are no hard lumps to potentially choke on. Finally, I will introduce staples like brown rice and potato, mixed in with the meat and vegetables.

Introduce one food at a time so you can watch out for any allergic reactions. If your baby develops hives or has a sudden attack of vomiting or diarrhea, take her to the hospital straight away.

Tip: Feed yourself
Many mothers say that they've never experienced such intense hunger or thirst as when they were breastfeeding. You may want to keep a liter bottle of water by the bed so that you don't have to fumble your way downstairs after a night feed. Stay away from caffeine, alcohol, and spicy foods. Keep an eye out for any food that upsets your baby's tummy and cut it out of your diet for the time being.

Here's a list of foods you should never give your baby:

- **UNCOOKED FOOD** Babies who haven't cut any teeth can't cope with raw food. Pieces might break off and choke them. Wait until your child is well over a year before giving her raw food, and supervise her closely when you do.
- **SEEDS AND NUTS** Seeds and nuts can also cause choking – make sure you deseed any fruit you offer. Many types of nut cause allergic reactions – avoid at all costs.
- **CITRUS FRUITS** like lemons and limes are too acidic for a baby's tummy.
- **SALT** Never add salt to a baby's diet. It puts strain on the kidneys.
- **SUGAR** No extra sugar or sugary treats, please! Fruit and vegetables contain natural sugars that are more than enough and are healthy.
- **COW'S MILK** Don't introduce cow's milk until your baby is at least a year old.
- **EGGS** Wait until your baby is a year old before giving her eggs. Egg whites, in particular, can cause an allergic reaction. You can feed her scrambled egg yolk at about nine months.
- **WHEAT** Watch out for wheat, which causes allergies in some children.
- **SHELLFISH** There's always the risk of food poisoning with shellfish. Don't offer shellfish to any children under two.

Q *My baby is six months old and he's just not interested in solid food at all. Every time I offer it to him, he spits it out again. I'm still breastfeeding him, and I've heard that breastfed babies take longer to get onto solids. Is this true? I'm worried that he's not getting enough to eat.*

A Weaning a baby onto solid foods takes time. Don't expect him to get the hang of it straight away. A couple of spoonfuls once a day is more than enough for him at the very beginning. Only introduce a second meal once he's taking a dozen spoonfuls or so at a time. As a rule of thumb, I use the plastic lid of a baby's milk bottle to measure out a portion size. A capful is a good start.

A baby doesn't spit food out because he doesn't like it. What happens is that when you put a spoonful of a new taste into his mouth, he explores it, pushing the food around with his tongue. This naturally waters down the food and out it dribbles onto his face and bib. Remember, milk is what he's used to. Solid food not only tastes different, it also has a different texture. Allow him some time to get used to the sensation. Up to now, he's been sucking – now he's got to learn to use a different muscle to eat his food.

At the same time, some tastes might just not appeal to him. If he turns his head away, or makes a disgusted face, that's a refusal. Don't force the issue. Try a different type of food the next time to see whether he likes it any better. Make sure that the food you offer your baby is not too hot. Warm is best.

Try giving him a plastic spoon to hang onto when you're feeding him. At five months, he's a long way off feeding himself, but he may enjoy waving it in the air and banging it on his tray. This can make mealtimes more fun for him.

If your baby has plenty of energy and is still gaining or maintaining his weight, he's getting the nutrition he needs. Make sure you offer him cooled, boiled water along with the breast so that he is not demanding a feed simply to quench his thirst.

There's no physical reason why weaning a baby who is breastfed should take longer than weaning a bottlefed baby. Sometimes, however, breastfed babies carry on wanting to suck because it is comforting to them. What they're doing is using the nipple as a pacifier. Sometimes Moms also find it difficult to wean a breastfed baby – the closeness they've enjoyed with their child is comforting for them, too. Weaning can be quite an emotional process on all sides. But take your time and remember that you will get there in the end.

Tip: Teething

Some babies are born with a tooth already cut. Most babies cut their first tooth sometime around three to six months. Others take longer. Here are the signs to watch out for whenever it occurs:

* *Red cheeks*
* *Biting down hard on everything*
* *Small, whitish bubbles on the gums*
* *A slight temperature – raised by no more than a degree*
* *Drooling*
* *Smellier diapers and sometimes a diaper rash*
* *Crying and waking at night*
* *Slight loss of appetite*

Soothe your baby with hard teething rings (frozen for extra relief), mild pain relievers or herbal remedies made especially for babies, and plenty of love and comfort.

F is for Fun.
Let your hair down and enjoy yourselves. Most of what kids learn, they learn through fun.

Q *I've been breastfeeding my son for nine months now and I'd like to stop, as I'm due to return to work soon. I'm not producing much milk any more, but he shows no sign of losing interest. I realize that he's getting comfort from sucking – sometimes it's the only way to soothe him, especially at night. How do I go about weaning him? He's been on solids for four and a half months.*

A Some babies wean themselves as soon as they're well established on solid foods. Others have to be coaxed into it. As you are no longer producing much milk and your son is eating well, you are going to have to point him in the right direction yourself. Your question screams out to me that you need to be reassured that it's the right time to do this. He's comfort-sucking. You have to break that tie and make the emotional change. You won't lose your bond with your child.

If he was younger, I would break him in gradually by cutting out the nighttime feeds, then move on to cutting the times you offer the breast in the day down to once in the morning and once last thing at night. Usually what happens is that a baby will then skip one of those daytime feeds, probably the one in the morning, which is the cue to stop breastfeeding altogether.

But in your case, I wouldn't go for the gradual route. As your son is nine months, sticking with the day nursing is only going to make your nights worse. The solution here is to stop breastfeeding altogether. As long as a child is offered the breast as a comforter, he will expect it. He's not going to suddenly refuse a pacifier that has always been there on demand!

If he finds it hard to settle without the breast, take a look at the chapter on Bedtimes (page 76). What your son needs to learn how to do is to initiate sleep himself and to settle himself back to sleep when he wakes. If he is waking repeatedly in the night and crying for attention, try the Controlled-Crying Technique (page 90).

Don't allow your son to fall asleep on the breast. When he gets sleepy, move him into his cot and encourage him to settle by himself. Make sure you offer your son plenty of fluids during the day, in the form of cooled, boiled water.

This cut-off point can be a very emotional time. Although you want to stop breast-feeding and have plenty of good reasons for wanting to do so, be prepared to feel a little twinge at the passing of this stage. Comfort yourself with the fact that your son is now ready to move on and so are you.

Tip: Burping
Most babies bring up a little milk. But if your baby takes in too much air with his milk, he might bring up the whole meal. If you are bottlefeeding, make sure the hole in the nipple is big enough to allow several drops of milk through per second, but not any bigger. Hold the bottle at an angle so that the air pocket does not reach the nipple. Try to burp your baby halfway through a feed. You can usually tell from their expression when they are full – their faces screw up in discomfort.

Q My two-and-a-half-year-old daughter is not interested in food. Everything I offer her, she refuses. She shouts "No!" and throws the food on the floor. All she wants to do is keep on drinking. I'm getting so stressed out about it I don't know what to do.

A Parents get themselves really worked up when their kids won't eat. Nothing is more guaranteed to send anxiety levels shooting off the scale. To set your mind at rest, I would suggest that you first take your daughter to the doctor and have her examined to eliminate any medical reason for her food refusal. Excessive thirst can be a sign of diabetes, especially if she is losing weight at the same time or shows signs of craving sugary foods. If she's within the normal weight range for a child her age, and she's reasonably energetic, then I think what you've got on your hands is a toddler who's using food as a means of control.

Many parents say that their kids won't eat, when what they mean is that they won't eat at mealtimes. Do you give her snacks at different times of the day? If you do, cut down on these so she is hungrier for her breakfast, lunch, and supper. What type of drinks do you offer her? Even juices are high in sugar, and can take the edge off a child's appetite. If you are giving her milk to drink throughout the day, she may be filling up on that. Offer her very diluted juice or water, and monitor her fluid intake.

How is she sleeping? If she has sleep problems, try to address these at the same time. A child who sleeps poorly often eats poorly, too. If you can get her into a better nighttime routine, you may find that her appetite improves.

Food refusal is common with this age group. Your stress at mealtimes will be obvious to her. She's getting attention for her behavior, even if it's negative attention. Stick to your mealtime routines. Sit down to eat with her. Don't offer her choices or bargain with her. If possible, try to arrange it so that you eat the same food as she does.

Make sure you give her a small portion. I'm constantly amazed how much food some parents pile on the plates of their toddlers. Kids find huge portions off-putting. A good-sized portion of food for a toddler is roughly what would fit on a side plate.

If she throws the food or shouts "No!," use one of the discipline techniques outlined in the chapter The Naughty Step and Beyond (page 168). Explain to her that shouting and throwing food is not allowed. Put your boundaries in place and choose your battles. You can be sure she's using food as a control issue if she's displaying similar behavior in other areas – refusing to get dressed, for example.

If she carries on refusing the food – compromise. Tell her she can leave the table when she has had three spoonfuls. Follow through – don't relax the rules when she's had one or two. Three spoonfuls means three spoonfuls. Praise her when she eats. Go over the top and make it clear how pleased you are. What you want to do is replace the negative attention she is getting for her food refusal with positive attention. Encouragement goes a long way toward correcting this behavior. So reward her.

Tip: Supper time!
*Give your kids an advance
warning when a meal is
coming up. "Supper in ten
minutes!" "Supper in five
minutes. Please wash your
hands!" Don't expect them
to drop what they're doing
and run to the table instantly.
Give them time to prepare
themselves for the change
in activity.*

Keep offering variety at each mealtime.
Once you have got her into a better eating
pattern, you may notice that there are some
foods that she just doesn't care for. Try
offering these in a different form to see if it's
the texture that bothers her rather than the
taste. For example, some kids like cooked
carrots but not raw ones, or vice versa.

Perseverance is the key here. Keep your
anxiety levels under control so that your
daughter isn't tempted to carry on turning
eating into a battle of wills.

Q *Mealtimes are crazy in our house. We've got three kids, aged nine, five, and four, and every time we sit down to eat together, it's complete and utter chaos. Millie, the nine-year-old, eats about half of what I give her and then disappears to watch TV. The other two are always fighting and acting up. What do I do? I don't want to act the heavy. Things are bad enough as they are.*

A And they're only going to get worse if you don't step up to the plate here (if you will excuse the pun) and show your children how you expect them to behave. Parents are often reluctant to discipline their kids over mealtime issues because a) they're focused on getting their kids to eat, and b) discipline disrupts an occasion that should be pleasurable. But bad behavior at the table is no different from bad behavior anywhere else. You need to agree on some clear rules with your partner and communicate these to your kids.

Why does your oldest daughter leave half her food? Are you giving her too much at a time? Don't pile her plate high. Give her a sensible portion. If she finishes that and wants more, give her more within reason. Teach your daughter to *ask* to be excused from the table when she's finished. Provided she doesn't gobble her food down in her haste to get away from the table, don't make her sit there for ages while the little ones finish. It isn't necessary.

If she's leaving her food to get back to the TV, that's a different matter. The TV should be off during meals. Full stop. Tell her she can leave the table provided the TV stays off until you say so. Remind her that there won't be more to eat until the next mealtime.

But I wouldn't be at all surprised if the major reason your daughter is so anxious to leave the table is to get away from her fighting siblings. Mealtimes aren't any more pleasant for her than they are for you. If you went out to eat at a restaurant, and the couple at the table next to you were going at it hammer and tongs, you wouldn't enjoy the occasion, would you? You'd go home with indigestion rather than a happy memory.

Use the Naughty-Step Technique or one of its variations (page 172) to get mealtimes back on track. When your warring kids act up at the table, insist that they stick to the rules and follow up any repeat performances with discipline. Things may get worse before they get better, but if you don't use discipline, they'll never improve.

Once you start to see better behavior at the table, you'll have the chance to talk to your kids and enjoy a relaxing time with them. And your nine-year-old won't be so desperate to run off and sit in front of the TV.

Tip: Seconds, please!
If your child finishes her plate and wants more, that's fine, within limits. But don't praise a child for eating a second helping. This sends out the wrong message. It's good to have a healthy appetite, and you'll be pleased that your home cooking has been appreciated, but eating two helpings should not be associated in your child's mind with behaving well.

Q *My son, who's three, won't eat vegetables. He used to eat pretty much whatever we gave him, but recently he's been saying that he hates peas, carrots, beans . . . The list seems to grow longer every day. I keep telling him how important it is to eat vegetables, but he just says he hates them.*

A All kids have likes and dislikes. It's only natural. Most parents do, too. Fussy eating is something different. While your son is not a full fledged fussy eater, he's heading that way, because you're allowing him to. Maybe he's worked out that rejecting food gets him attention, or maybe it just means that if he leaves his vegetables he can get on with doing whatever he wants to do quicker. Nip things in the bud now, before he moves onto another food group!

Offer him a choice of vegetables with each meal. If he refuses to eat what he's chosen, remind him that he made his choice and ask him to have a couple of spoonfuls.

Don't overreact to the refusals. Many small children will announce that they hate a certain kind of food and then eat the same thing happily when it's offered to them a few months later, particularly if the refusal received no attention. Toddlers aren't particularly consistent with their likes and dislikes: "I *like* tomatoes now!" they will announce proudly, three days after they've told you they hate them. Try offering raw vegetables – sometimes it's not the taste, it's the texture that kids don't like. Or you could mix vegetables in with a stew or shepherd's

pie. And don't offer too many choices ("Cabbage? Broccoli? Green beans?") – this will only give him the opportunity to add new things to his list of rejects.

At the same time, be on the lookout for food that he really does hate. Genuine disgust is hard to fake or conceal – it will be written all over his face. If he really does hate peas, keep peas off the menu. Try not to communicate your own likes and dislikes while you're at it. You may not be that keen on mushrooms, but there's no reason why you shouldn't offer them to your son. We often influence our kids without realizing it, just by the way we react. Personally, I don't like liver, but I would always offer it as a tasty dish.

Q *My five-year-old daughter Amy has always been a poor eater. But things have got really bad lately and she's refusing to eat anything except plain pasta with a little grated cheese on top. If we put anything else in front of her, she screams and won't even touch it. She starts school in a couple of months and I'm so worried what's going to happen at dinnertime – I can't bear to think of her going all day without anything in her tummy. Please help.*

A Most kids go through phases of eating less than usual, or phases of eating the same food over and over again. If you don't call attention to the behavior or overreact, it usually passes in a short space of time.

Your daughter's behavior tells me that she has learned over the years to use food as an issue of control. You need to address this situation right away before it gets any worse than it already is.

How do you act when she refuses food? Do you plead with her? Do you get cross? Do you try to force her to eat? The first thing you've got to do is take the emotional heat out of mealtimes. I can tell that your daughter's eating habits are really worrying you. That's understandable. All parents panic when their kids don't eat properly. But to get her back to a healthy pattern of eating, you've got to stop giving her attention for her negative behavior. At the same time, you also have to stop pandering to her limited diet and instead offer her a variety of balanced meals. Once she starts to eat, even if she manages only a single mouthful of a different kind of food, give her plenty of praise.

There's no quick fix to fussy eating, especially if the pattern has been going on for some time. It will take a lot of patience and determination on your part to turn things around. But whatever you do, don't fall back on offering her what she was eating before just because you can't cope with the anxiety and frustration you feel when she eats next to nothing. If you persevere, it will get better, bite by bite, step by step.

One of the worst cases of fussy eating I've ever had to deal with was a seven-year-old boy who was almost food-phobic. By the time I visited the family, the little boy ate fries and little else. His behavior was OK, but he was tired all the time, partly because he just wasn't getting the nourishment he needed. His parents could trace his issues with food back to a bad case of gastric flu that their son had had as a baby. *Six years later*, mealtimes were a real struggle for Mom and Dad. Their child wouldn't touch, let alone taste, most of the food he was offered. His parents had lost all patience with his lack of enthusiasm for eating, and the situation had spiraled into a negative pattern with huge amounts of destructive energy and attention focused on mealtimes. He would go for days hardly eating, until his parents would give in and offer him junk food in a desperate attempt to get him to eat something.

The parents' feelings of anger and frustration came from the fact that they knew he was perfectly happy to eat fast food when he was ready.

On the next pages are some of the ways I dealt with the situation.

Below are some of the techniques I used to get to work on that child's food-phobia. Try them and I'm sure you'll start to see improvements:

★ **The Good-Eater Technique** One of the first things I did with that family was to get them to chuck out the fries pan and shop for healthy food that Mom and Dad would actually have to cook, rather than heat up. Then I got Mom and Dad to sit down and draw up two menus for the main meal of the day. They wrote the choices down on two paper plates and asked the kids to choose which dinner they wanted.

At first their eldest son didn't want to engage at all and refused both of the choices, but his little brother picked the one he liked the sound of and that was what the family had for dinner. After a few dinners, the older boy felt able to join in and express a preference himself.

When a child is refusing all food, offering her a limited choice between two healthy alternatives gives her a say in the matter so she doesn't feel she's being forced to eat something that you have told her to. It is important to bear in mind that the choices you offer should be healthy alternatives that you want your child to eat. What you shouldn't do is offer her only what she is prepared to eat.

★ If your child still refuses to eat, encourage her to try one mouthful of food. Don't nag or order her. Once she takes a little bite, give her plenty of praise to continue the good eating behavior.

★ If your child still refuses to take a mouthful, don't overreact. Make sure she knows that she will get nothing else to eat until the next meal. Then cut off a little piece of food that you want her to eat. Encourage her to eat that piece. At this stage, it isn't about getting the child to finish her plate, it's about getting her to try new foods.

★ **Placemat Reward Chart** You can try using a Placemat Reward Chart for positive feedback. I did this for that seven-year-old and his brother. The placemat had four sections around the edge, two on each side: one for protein (red), one for carbohydrate (blue), one for fruit (yellow), and one for vegetables (green). He and his little brother got a different color sticker each time they took a mouthful of a food group. If they ate a whole portion, they got a smiley face. Both parents were encouraged to give their elder son plenty of praise the first time he tried something new. As time went by and he got more adventurous, I asked Mom and Dad to scale down the praise for each mouthful, so that he could learn that eating well was no big deal. When he managed to finish a portion, they could carry on praising as usual.

★ I also used the **Little-Chef Technique** (page 60) to get the kids involved in cooking, encourage bonding, and help the elder boy get over his fear of food. I dressed the kids up in chef's hats and aprons and got them busy – mixing, making smoothies, writing menus, and generally helping to get the dinner ready. They got plenty of praise for their efforts. What do chefs do? They taste as they go along to see how the dish is turning out. Before long, he was licking his fingers.

★ **Taking responsibility** In addition, I gave him a tomato plant to help teach him that all growing things need to be fed, loved, and taken care of. He was in charge of the plant and had to feed it with compost and keep it watered and cared for. After a few weeks, he was proud of all the new healthy foods he had tried, and his parents were able to report that he was happier all around and had much more energy for playing and having fun.

Be realistic in your expectations. Turning around a food disorder takes time. Don't be impatient for instant change and do continue to acknowledge progress, even if it is slow and small. If your child refuses point-blank to eat, clear the plate away at the end of the meal and don't offer anything else. Your daughter must get the idea that she cannot make up for missed meals by snacking or having treats.

Eating disorders of all kinds are on the increase, and they're showing up in younger and younger children – of both sexes. Kids as young as eight, nine, and ten are bombarded by media images of airbrushed pop stars and celebrities setting seemingly impossible standards of physical perfection. This naturally affects their confidence and self-esteem. Take every opportunity to ease the pressure on your kids and teach them that it's the beauty inside that counts. Remind them that the popular girl at school has flaws as well, and that no one's perfect. If you suspect your child is developing serious issues with food, the faster you act, the better. Don't wait for it to go away. Seek advice from your doctor or a therapist, or contact an eating disorders association for advice. These illnesses are not about food, they're about feelings and false images.

KEY POINT

Sit down together as a family for meals and talk about what you've all been doing that day. Focusing too much on a fussy eater and what she is or isn't eating sends the wrong message. Have a conversation about something apart from food – show your kids that mealtimes can be fun and relaxing, and not a source of anxiety.

Tip: Convenience food
Find the time to have fun cooking food with your children. Involve them; they'll be more interested.

Q *My four-year-old daughter has started begging for snacks just before she goes to bed. I don't want her to fill up on junk, but my husband says I'm being too strict and the odd chocolate cookie or bag of chips is not going to do her any harm. Am I being unreasonable? Should I let her eat what she wants?*

A Snacks can play a positive role in children's diets. A little boost of energy after active play, and extra nutrition or fluid intake between meals is all well and good, within reason. Three meals a day is roughly an adult pattern of eating. Small kids often benefit from a small snack mid-morning and mid-afternoon. But it's important to keep your eye on the quantity so that you don't spoil their appetites for the main meals of the day.

It's a case of quality as well as quantity. Healthy snacks such as yogurt, cubes of cheese, fruit, raw vegetables, and diluted fruit juice are great. Fizzy soft drinks, chips, cookies, and sweets, on the other hand, have little nutritional value. I'm not saying you should never let kids have these kinds of snacks, but they shouldn't be on constant offer. Everything in moderation. Food and drink that is high in sugar sends kids' blood sugar levels through the roof. The sugar rush takes them in different ways – running around, shouting, acting silly, being aggressive – as if they're punch-drunk. Remind you of anything? Think of the average birthday party. Then, after the sugar rush, blood sugar levels take a nose dive, dropping even lower than they were before the sugary

snack. Whining, tantrums, and other kinds of bad behavior will follow. Chocolate last thing at night isn't so smart. An instant sugar high isn't the best way to wind your child down for bed. What you've got here is a bad habit. And it's up to you to break it.

I saw a vivid illustration of this in one of the families I worked with. The Youngs were really struggling to bring their five boys under nine under control. Mob rule is a polite term for what was going on in that house. The boys fought, spat, swore, dug up the garden with spoons, broke things, punched holes in doors . . . I helped the family implement some basic discipline techniques and things began to improve. Then, one evening after a day when the boys had made a real effort to get on top of their behavior, Dad came home from work and decided to treat them – to a huge bag of sweets. Five boys under nine in the grip of a massive sugar rush isn't a pretty sight, I can tell you!

Something similar was going on in the Ririe household. When I opened a pantry door in their kitchen, I couldn't believe my eyes. It was Candy Land in there, and the kids had access to it 24/7. Small wonder that they had no appetite for their meals or that their behavior was challenging. What I did in that case was to introduce the **Snack-Jar Technique**.

Each child was given their own snack jar and allowed to choose three healthy snacks to put into it. A household routine was drawn up with allocated snack times. If the kids ate all the snacks in their jars before the day was over, no other snacks were offered.

You and your husband are also going to have to find some common ground here. Use the Same-Page Technique (page 30) to resolve your differences in this area.

Here are my rules for snacks:

* Offer small children a healthy snack mid-morning and mid-afternoon. Don't give sugar fixes.
* Restrict access to snacks so kids can't help themselves. Put snacks away and keep them out of reach.
* Watch the quantities you give. Don't give huge snacks that take away your child's appetite for main meals.
* Don't allow snacks close to mealtimes.
* Don't use snacks as a bribe or as a way of bargaining with kids to eat properly.
* Treats are fine from time to time, but give them on your terms.

Tip: Snack time
Use your common sense about snacks. If you were delayed in the morning for some reason and the routine has gone out of the window, skip the morning snack. That way your kids will still have a good appetite for lunch.

Tip: Sugar highs and lows
Sugar in the body is broken down by a hormone called insulin, which is produced in the pancreas. When a child eats a sugary snack or drinks a sugary drink, blood sugar levels soar into the stratosphere. That stimulates the pancreas to produce more and more insulin to break the sugar down. The result of that is a rapid drop in blood sugar levels. These highs and lows show up in dramatic mood swings – excess energy when blood sugar is high, irritability and whining when it's low. Complex carbohydrates, such as whole grains and root vegetables, release their sugar content slowly, which means blood sugar levels remain steady through the day.

G is for Grandparents.
It's a true special relationship. Grandparents play such an important role in the family dynamic – they've earned it!

3 Bedtimes

In many families, bedtime is a major trigger point for chaos and disruption. Getting the kids to bed and keeping them there can take all night when there are no set routines and no firm controls in place. The next day, exhausted parents and children are like a time bomb waiting to go off.

Last year I worked alongside the American National Sleep Foundation when they were conducting a survey on sleep behavior in children. The results, which were released in October 2005, were very revealing. Here are some of the findings:

★ 40% of the parents and caregivers who answered the survey said that their infants and toddlers were sleeping less than the 12–15 hours per day recommended by the NSF and pediatric sleep experts.

★ 40% said that their children had a sleep problem every night.

★ 64% said that their infants and toddlers exhibited a sleep behavior problem that interfered with them getting the recommended amount of sleep at least a few times a week.

★ 25% of parents and caregivers surveyed said that their infants, toddlers, and preschoolers appeared sleepy or tired during the day.

★ 34% believed that a child's sleep pattern could impact and disrupt the entire family.

★ 71% of the parents and caregivers who responded said they got less sleep than they needed.

★ 98% agreed that children are happier after a good night's sleep.

These responses came from *parents* and other caregivers involved with children. Why are these results so worrying?

Think about it for a minute. How do you feel when you haven't had enough rest? Without enough sleep, we can't function well the next day, we're groggy and irritable, our reactions are slower, our levels of concentration are poor. If that continues night after night, our immune systems begin to suffer and we are more likely to pick up colds and feel rundown. We're also more likely to have accidents. The consequences of sleep deprivation can be serious. After all, it's a torture technique.

It's no different for children, and in some ways it's worse. Children need much more sleep than adults because they're growing and developing, both mentally and physically. And, unlike adults, who can have a nap or a rest, children who are put to bed too late or who only manage to settle down after hours of resistance won't be able to make up the shortfall the next day. You may well have noticed that if your child has a late night, it doesn't affect what time he wakes up the next morning. What it does affect is his behavior, his appetite, and his mood. And then yours, as well. Let's face it, it's the domino effect.

Sleep problems affect many families. They are one of the most common reasons why parents seek professional help and advice. Many problems that families suffer, particularly behavioral ones, are made worse and may even be caused by the fact that children are not getting enough sleep. A child who is overtired is a child who has a short fuse the whole of the next day, which often results in more frequent tantrums, squabbling, or other outbursts of bad behavior, including trouble at school. Once a settled bedtime routine is put in place, other problem areas often improve dramatically, as if by magic.

Tip: *Catch the moment*

Some parents think that if they keep a child up a little later, she will be more likely to go to sleep, because she will have well and truly tired herself out. The opposite is the case. Kids who are overtired get wound up and find it harder to settle. Catch the right moment – which is often earlier than you think – and you're halfway there.

Look for the telltale signs – tired eyes, rubbing ears, sucking thumbs, yawning – it's all in the body language.

What causes sleep problems?

"Lots of things," is the answer, but very rarely what parents suppose. Many parents find it difficult to get their kids to go to bed. But they see it differently. "My son doesn't need as much sleep as other kids." "My daughter has never been a good sleeper." "My boys are just too lively to go to bed without a fight." These aren't reasons, they're excuses. I would bet money that those same children who are poor sleepers would become good sleepers given the chance – if, for example, there were established mealtimes and a consistent bedtime routine.

Here are some reasons why families develop sleep problems:

★ **GUILT** In families where both parents work, sometimes there's a lot of guilt confusing the issue. You go to work all day and you're beginning to realize that your workload means that you are leaving earlier in the morning and getting home later. You miss your kids – of course you do. So when you come home it's tempting to let them stay up longer, so you can have more time with them. Then bedtimes get pushed back later and later. Both parents don't have to work for this to be the case. Dads who can't make it back in time for their kids' mealtimes may let their kids stay up later for the same reason. There is a price to pay. You shouldn't adjust your kids' bedtimes to suit you. They need their sleep even more than you do.

★ **TIREDNESS** Tiredness breeds tiredness (as well as digestive problems, poor concentration, increased stress, and other negative things). Looking after children can be exhausting at the best of times. If you're below par and haven't slept well yourself, or haven't managed to get the rest you need, or the time off you need to recharge your batteries, it's going to be more difficult to enforce a bedtime routine because you won't have the stamina. You might be tempted to skip a stage or rush things along – or the routine might just stretch out over too long a period so that you miss the moment when your child would have dropped off to sleep easily. Now you've got a battle on your hands – without the reserves to deal with it. And the kids are overtired, too.

★ **BAD HABITS** You brought your daughter into your bed a couple of times, and now she won't sleep anywhere else. All parents make mistakes. The thing is to learn from them and then move on. Patterns that don't work for you and your kids can be changed. It just takes time and perseverance.

★ **CONVENIENCE** I'm sorry to say it, but it's true. It takes effort to enforce a bedtime routine and some parents give up at the first hurdle. Rather than return a child to bed, they take the easy way out and let their child stay up, or let them climb into bed with them and snuggle down under the covers. Except that, in the long run, this isn't the easy way out at all, is it?

* **"ANYTHING FOR A QUIET NIGHT!"** Responding to bedtime tantrums or screaming matches by letting your kids get out of bed or stay up is not an easy way out, either. What you have taught your kids is that tantrums work and they will repeat the performance to get the result they want.

* **BEING TOO UPTIGHT** All parents are wired to respond to their children's needs. If you can't bear to hear your baby cry for a second – even the sounds that many babies make just before they drop off to sleep – but hover anxiously or rush to pick him up and soothe him, he may find it hard to learn how to go to sleep by himself. You need to teach a baby to initiate sleep by himself. The new baby monitors that come with cameras and screens can feed these kinds of anxieties. I've seen parents looking at those monitors 24/7 – they're not listening and learning how to distinguish between a cry of distress or pain and the ordinary sounds babies make; instead, they're *watching*. Technology can prevent parents from learning the skills they need.

* **LACK OF CONFIDENCE** Kids who are running circles around their parents every night often do so because parents lack the confidence to assert their authority and take control of the situation. Children do not instinctively know what's best: they have to be shown and taught what to do. You set their bedtimes: It's not up to them.

* **DIFFERING STYLES OF PARENTING** Mom wants the kids in bed, but Dad says it's OK for them to stay up just this once and watch TV. Kids pick up on mixed messages fast. It's the thin end of the wedge. If you don't agree as parents, expect your kids to play you against one another or take no notice of you altogether.

* **LACK OF CONSISTENCY** Monday night you were firm about bedtime. Tuesday your friend came around for supper and you relaxed the rules. A bedtime routine isn't a routine if it's all over the place.

I could go on, if you've got an extra day or two and if your eyelids aren't drooping already, but you get the picture. A child's sleep problem, particularly one that's become a pattern over weeks or months, is more often than not of a parent's making.

BUT

Not always. Here are some other reasons why you might be having broken or difficult nights because your child won't sleep:

* **PAIN OR DISCOMFORT,** caused by teething, for example (page 64). Ear infections can be excruciatingly painful and can affect sleep.

* **BEDWETTING** Sometimes a child will wake up as soon as she wets the bed; sometimes it's the chill as the urine evaporates that wakes her up.

★ **ILLNESS** Fevers, colds, stomachaches, as well as common childhood illnesses, can throw a routine out the window for a while.

★ **TRAVEL**, especially flights across time zones. Small children are ill-equipped to cope with the effects of jet lag. Long car or train journeys can also disrupt timetables – your child may sleep most of the trip or miss out on naps completely. Both will affect nighttime routines.

★ **STRANGE BEDS** Children are highly territorial and love the security of their own beds. Take some familiar toys with you when you go away – as well as a pillow and blanket if you have the space – to ease the transition.

★ **FEARS AND PHOBIAS** Many children go through a short-lived phase when they are frightened at night.

★ **NIGHTMARES**

★ **TENSION IN THE FAMILY** during periods of stress.

★ **DISRUPTION TO NORMAL SCHEDULES** – for example, a parent returning to work after maternity/paternity leave.

★ **NEW DEVELOPMENTAL STAGES** You may notice a period of wakefulness when your child starts to walk, for example.

★ **A NEW HOME OR ENVIRONMENT** that places the child in a different space.

In most of these cases, once you identify the cause, and deal with it appropriately, you should be able to get things back on track in a relatively short space of time. Whatever the reason for the sleep problem, I'll be covering a range of techniques in this chapter to help your family enjoy quiet, peaceful nights.

Topics and techniques covered in this chapter:

GOOD-SLEEP PATTERN to encourage babies to sleep through

SAFE-SLEEP RULES to cut the risk of SIDS (Sudden Infant Death Syndrome)

BEDTIME ROUTINE for a calm winding-down to bed

THE CONTROLLED-CRYING TECHNIQUE to settle babies and toddlers back to sleep

TO NAP OR NOT

THE MAGIC-DUST TECHNIQUE for fears and nightmares

THE STAY-IN-BED TECHNIQUE for children who repeatedly get out of bed

SHARING A BED – yes or no?

THE CHIMES TECHNIQUE to alert you to nighttime disturbances

THE SLEEP-SEPARATION TECHNIQUE for children who can't get to sleep by themselves

THE ELEVENISH-GET-UP-TO-PEE TECHNIQUE to prevent bedwetting

SLEEP-INS AND EARLY WAKING

Tip: Deep sleep
*Sleep is not just important for a child's
health and wellbeing, it's necessary
for growth. Deep sleep (non-dreaming
sleep) is when growth hormones are
released. So it's true when you tell your
seven-year-old: 'If you get plenty of sleep,
you'll grow up into a big, strong boy!'
About half the time babies spend asleep
should be spent in deep sleep, not in
the kind of shallow sleep they get
in babychairs.*

Q *I'm expecting my first baby in two months' time. I've heard a lot of horror stories from my friends about sleepless nights. One mother I know hasn't had an unbroken night for two years! I've always needed a lot of sleep myself, so I'm worrying about how I'm going to cope. Are there any techniques you know to help babies sleep through the night, or should I just accept I'm going to be pretty tired for a while and try to get through it somehow?*

A Please don't be discouraged by the horror stories. No one says having a baby, particularly your first, is not challenging. At the same time, it's one of the most beautiful experiences anyone can have. The important thing is to approach it in a positive way. Congratulations and well done for trying to prepare yourself as much as possible before the event.

The first few weeks after birth are an emotional roller coaster for most new parents. I'm not promising you that you won't be tired in the early days, because you will. For that reason, it's important to make sure you have support from your partner – or anyone else who can help you – to enable you to get enough rest. That way you can look after the little one and keep on top of things at home as much as possible. This will make the transition a much easier ride.

Sleepless nights are what all new parents dread. The good news is that there is a lot you can do right from the start that will help settle your baby into a good sleep pattern:

★ A newborn baby needs between 16 and 18 hours of sleep every 24 hours. In the first weeks, this will be more or less evenly divided between night and day. By six months to nine months, the amount of sleep she needs will have dropped slightly to 12–15 hours. If you have set up a good routine, most of that sleep should be at nighttime, supplemented by two or three daytime naps.

★ Very young babies can only take in so much milk at a time, and will wake up when they are hungry and sometimes when they are wet. Their sleep cycles are also much shorter than ours. One of the most important things to teach your baby is how to learn to fall asleep by herself so that when she does wake up, she can settle or soothe herself back to sleep again after she has been fed or changed. We adults wake up in the night, too, but the difference is that we barely register these moments of consciousness unless there's a lot on our minds (or a noisy party next door!).

★ In the very early stages, you should keep your baby's bassinet or cot in your room so you can respond when she wakes to nurse. But by around three to six months, she should be in a room of her own if possible. (If you are finding it hard not to respond to every little noise she makes, you may well find a baby monitor a mixed blessing unless you are several flights of stairs away and wouldn't hear her crying otherwise.)

★ From about six weeks onward, try to put your baby to bed before she's actually asleep. She should be drowsy and relaxed, but not fully asleep. This applies whether you are breastfeeding or bottlefeeding. There's a knack to it – you have to get the timing right – but it is worth persevering. A baby who learns to drift off to sleep by herself without the comfort of falling to sleep in your arms will be much easier to settle later on.

★ Encourage her to sleep longer at nighttime by making sure lights are off or very dimmed. A nightlight will allow you to see your way to her cot without telling her it's time to wake up. Don't bring her downstairs into a brightly lit room. Feed her, but don't talk to her, sing to her, or play with her. Keep everything low-key and avoid full eye contact as much as possible – look at the bridge of her nose instead. The more attention you pay to her at night, beyond what is strictly necessary, the more incentive she has to wake up. So create a calm and tranquil setting.

★ Once your baby's body clock develops and a routine becomes more established, she will nap at similar times of the day. This means you can take her out in the stroller and meet a friend for lunch, say, without worrying that you will disrupt her routine. Lay the stroller back in the reclining position, pull the hood over to darken it a little, and make sure she has her comforter. She should drop off at the usual time – you don't have to rush back home to put her in her cot.

★ It's very tempting to let babies nap on and on during the day – after all, it gives you time to rest yourself or get on with the chores. But so does putting an established routine in place. Babies need plenty of naptime, but they also need to learn the difference between day and night. If your baby's nap is turning into a real marathon session (more than three hours, for example), wake her up. Your baby needs mental stimulation during the day, not at night. (It's also important to bear in mind that one reason a baby may nap for longer is because she's ill. If you suspect she's coming down with something, take her to the doctor.)

★ Use extra absorbent diapers at nighttime so you don't have to change her unnecessarily (and wake her in the process). If she's soiled herself and uncomfortable, or soaking wet, of course you should change her, but she doesn't need to be changed every time she wakes.

★ From an early age, help her to settle at night by introducing a bedtime routine as early as you can. Bathe her – warm water is naturally relaxing – cuddle her and feed her. Baby massage and aromatherapy are great, too. Even young babies respond to a sleeping pattern. Keep to set times and make sure the routine is as consistent as possible.

★ Make sure her room is not too hot. A cooler temperature at night encourages sleep. Dress her in a sleep suit and cover her in thin layers, so you can peel off a cover if she's too warm.

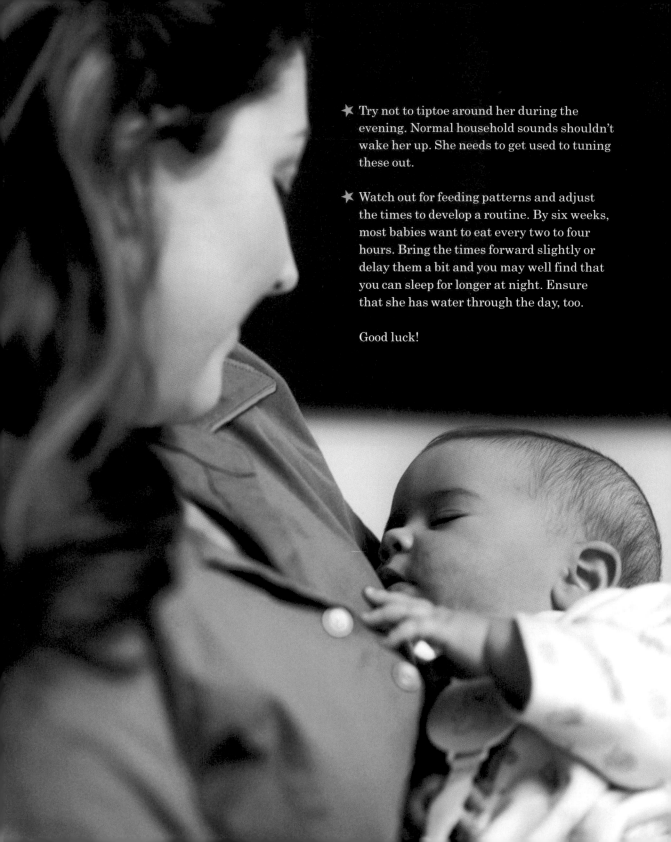

★ Try not to tiptoe around her during the evening. Normal household sounds shouldn't wake her up. She needs to get used to tuning these out.

★ Watch out for feeding patterns and adjust the times to develop a routine. By six weeks, most babies want to eat every two to four hours. Bring the times forward slightly or delay them a bit and you may well find that you can sleep for longer at night. Ensure that she has water through the day, too.

Good luck!

Q *What's the safest way of putting a baby to bed? I've heard that you should always put your baby down on her back. I'm expecting our third next month, but I always put our other two down on their tummies, and they never came to any harm.*

A The safest way for a baby to sleep is on her back. For the first six months, you should always put a baby down on her back; after that she should be able to roll over, and although you may start her on her back, you will probably find that she changes positions during the night.

Some babies like to be swaddled. In this case, you can roll a blanket into a sausage shape and wedge it down one side to keep her from rolling onto her tummy.

A lot of research has been carried out to determine the safest ways for babies to sleep. Most experts now agree that babies who sleep on their tummies are at greatest risk of cot death or SIDS. In many countries, including Britain, the United States, France, Norway, Sweden, Australia, and New Zealand, SIDS is the leading cause of death in babies between the ages of one month and one year. Recent research has identified a number of ways in which you can reduce the risk significantly.

Safe-Sleeping Rules (according to the Foundation for the Study of Infant Deaths):

★ **ALWAYS PUT BABIES DOWN ON THEIR BACKS** Before an infant can roll over, she might suffocate or overheat in a face-down position.

★ **DON'T PUT A PILLOW IN THE BED** until a baby is over a year old, if at all.

★ **ALWAYS MAKE SURE THE SHEET FIT SECURELY ON THE CRIB,** so there is no room for the baby to wriggle down under the bedclothes.

★ **ALWAYS USE FITTED UNDERSHEETS** Many experts recommend that you avoid covering babies with blankets until they are over a year. If you do want to cover your baby, choose a thin blanket, pulled up no higher than the chest, and tuck it in carefully. Otherwise, keep the baby warm in a sleep suit.

★ **KEEP THE ROOM RELATIVELY COOL** Overheating increases the dangers. But don't let a baby get too cold.

★ **MATTRESSES SHOULD BE FIRM,** not soft or sagging. Don't use secondhand mattresses unless you know where they've come from.

★ **NEVER SMOKE AROUND YOUR BABY** Mothers and fathers who smoke pose a serious risk to their children. Give it up now!

★ **IF YOU HAVE BEEN DRINKING, SMOKING, OR TAKING DRUGS,** sharing a bed with your infant also increases the risk of SIDS. Small babies are more likely to overheat in adult beds.

Q *Bedtimes are a nightmare in our household. It can take up to three hours to settle our three kids for the night, by which time I'm absolutely exhausted and at the end of my tether. We've got two boys aged seven and five, and a little girl who's two and a half. I try to get my daughter to bed first while the boys play and watch TV with their Dad, but by the time she's in her cot, the other two have usually started squabbling (they fight a lot). Then the next thing I know, my daughter has woken up and is crying to be picked up. The other night she managed to climb out of her cot. Darren, the eldest, is rarely asleep before 10:00 p.m. Some nights my husband and I never get any free time at all. I absolutely dread the evenings.*

A I'm not surprised – sleep deprivation has become your new best friend! Your whole family is feeling the strain.

It sounds to me like you're struggling to manage chaos without getting on top of the situation. I think it's clear that the pair of you – you *and* your husband – need to work together to establish a decent bedtime routine for all three kids. You both need to put in the time and effort to create a calm wind-down to bed. Even if you had just one child, both of you should still be taking turns to do bedtimes whenever possible; with three children, it's all the more important to share the load. You guys need to come together and work as a team.

All your kids are going to bed too late. Ten o'clock at night is *much* too late for a seven-year-old to be getting to sleep – he still needs between 10 and 12 hours sleep a night. And now that your toddler can climb out of her cot, you're going to have to set some boundaries or things are going to go from bad to worse really quickly.

What you need is a firm **Bedtime Routine**. This serves two purposes. First, it allows the children to unwind in a calm and peaceful atmosphere so that they are in the right frame of mind to go to bed. Second, it puts boundaries in place that you can enforce, which stops bedtime slipping later and later until it eats up the whole evening. Very few children are going to put their hands up and ask to go to bed. It's up to you to set the framework.

★ First of all, set a bedtime for each child. I would suggest 7:30 p.m. for your toddler and your four-year-old, and 8:00 p.m. for your eldest. Young children still need much more sleep than we do. Bring bedtimes forward rather than push them back, and you may be pleasantly surprised.

★ The entire bedtime routine for each child should take between half an hour to an hour, from getting into the bath to saying goodnight. Don't rush it or your children will feel short-changed, especially if you leave out a stage, but don't prolong it either.

★ As bedtime approaches, keep things as calm as possible. This means no noisy play, no competitive games or rough and tumble. It's OK to let older kids watch the TV for a little while, but don't let them get involved in a program that's going to finish after their bedtime – this will just become a bargaining point. And don't let them watch anything that is likely to wind them up too much or get them over-excited.

★ Let your children know when each stage of the routine is coming up: "It's time for a bath in ten minutes." "In three minutes, it's time to get out of the bath." "In two minutes, we're going to read a story." It's a running commentary, basically. Small children can't tell the time and have very little sense even of how long an hour is. Letting them know what's coming up helps them prepare for the next stage. Parents are always saying: "Quickly! Quickly! Hurry up and put your pajamas on!" No wonder their kids feel like they're being rushed from pillar to post and dig their heels in.

★ My guess is that your boys use fighting at bedtime as a stalling tactic. Plus, they're getting to bed so late, they're bound to be overtired. What they could do with at this point in the evening is some one-to-one attention. One way of giving them this is to separate them at bedtimes. You can get your four-year-old to help you bathe your daughter, for example. This will make him feel responsible – like a big boy. Praise him for helping you. "Can you fetch a towel for Mommy, please? Well done!" This way he

won't have the chance to squabble with his older brother. At the same time, your husband can be having some one-on-one time with your eldest.

★ After your toddler has finished her bath, and you've brushed her teeth and got her into her pajamas, settle down with her and read her a story. By this time, the older two can be having their bath.

★ Once you have settled your toddler, your husband can put your four-year-old to bed and read him a story while you spend some time with your eldest.

★ Try to vary the routine so that some nights your husband is putting the toddler to bed and you are responsible for the older boys. As well as easing the strain at the end of the day, this will allow each child to have undivided attention from each parent. A lot of bad behavior at bedtime is attention-seeking.

Tip: Lights out!
Don't leave bright lights (or candles!) on in children's rooms. If your child says she doesn't like the dark, you can use a nightlight, a lamp on a really low wattage, a mobile that projects light and shapes, or leave the door open a fraction. Anything brighter, and she will find it hard to get to sleep by herself. Darkness triggers the release of the sleep hormone melatonin.

Q My daughter is nine months old, and she's never slept through the night. She used to wake up a couple of times to nurse when I was breastfeeding, but now that she's weaned and on solids, she's waking up even more often, and it takes ages to get her back to sleep again. Is she hungry? Should I be offering her a bottle when she wakes up in the middle of the night?

A I wouldn't advise this for two reasons. Filling her up with milk at nighttime is bound to affect her appetite for solids during the day, which means she won't be getting the range of nutrients she needs at her age. More importantly, offering her a bottle when she wakes up at night will mean that she will begin to associate having a bottle with settling down, and won't learn how to get to sleep by herself. Plus, leaving a baby unsupervised in bed with a bottle can be dangerous – it's a choking hazard.

I very much doubt your baby is hungry. It's not uncommon for babies to eat a little less around the time they are a year old – the appetite just seems to taper off a bit. If she's active and thriving, chances are she's getting what she needs.

In other words, I don't think this is an eating problem at all. It's a sleeping problem.

I've noticed that at around nine months or so, babies who had been previously sleeping through the night start to wake up again. The same thing seems to happen just after the first year, at 13–14 months, and again at 18–20 months. For some reason, these periods also seem to coincide with times when babies are more clingy during the day. If your baby is waking now, but used to sleep through before, I would just say to persevere with the routine and this phase will pass. But if she has never slept through the night, you're going to have to try something different.

You don't mention how you respond when she wakes up. If you rush in to soothe her as soon as she cries, you may well be making matters worse. She cries and she gets your attention. That's a result! She cries again and here comes Mom . . . it's not going to take long before she's got that one worked out. Soothing your baby, picking her up, rocking her, talking to her – these are all welcome forms of attention as far as your baby is concerned. Before long, you may find yourself driving her around the block strapped in her car seat – anything to get her to drop off! It's not that she's being manipulative, she's just responding to a pattern that you are helping to create. Babies who have never learned to settle and soothe themselves to sleep, particularly babies who are used to dropping off to sleep while they are sucking on a bottle or breast, seem particularly prone to waking and crying in the night.

Nine months of broken nights is enough for anyone. You've got terrific stamina to have coped with it so long. But now it's time to take the opportunity to encourage your baby to settle by herself. A lot of parents find this hard to do, which is why some of them wind up years later at sleep clinics with four- and five-year-olds who still can't sleep through the night.

In any circumstance where repeated waking is taking its toll and the baby is well past weaning, I would recommend the **Controlled-Crying Technique**. I have always found this technique works extremely well, and can break a pattern of wakefulness in babies really quickly.

But before you go ahead and put the technique into practice, it's important to eliminate all the reasons why your baby might be crying at night. Run through the following checklist:

IS SHE WET?

IS SHE WELL ESTABLISHED ON SOLIDS? A baby has to be eating solid food before you use this technique, so you're sure it's not hunger.

DOES SHE HAVE AN ESTABLISHED ROUTINE? You need a pattern to work with.

IS SHE TEETHING? Signs include a baby who is off her food, smelly diapers, and red cheeks. Don't try the technique until she's cut the tooth.

IS SHE ILL? Has she been fretful or "off" during the day? Follow your gut instinct if you suspect something is not right. That instinct is there for a reason.

ARE YOU COPING REASONABLY WELL — apart from the sleepless nights, that is? If you are suffering from post-partum depression, or if you are on medication, I wouldn't advise trying the technique.

DOES SHE STOP CRYING WHEN YOU PICK HER UP? If she does, you'll know beyond the shadow of a doubt that she's crying for attention. Babies who are ill or in pain generally keep on crying. The exception is the baby who's worked herself up into such a state that she's not going to stop anytime soon.

HOW THE TECHNIQUE WORKS

All parents, particularly mothers, are programmed to respond to their child's cry. With this technique you have to steel yourself to ignore crying for limited periods of time, and this can be very demanding and draining. You'll need a lot of support to get through the negative emotions you might be feeling, such as panic and loss of control. But it is important to remember that this technique is not the same as "leaving a child to cry" or "letting a child cry it out." If your child cries night and day and gets no response whatsoever, that is abandonment and neglect. The difference with this technique is there in the word "controlled." Each time your child cries, you reassure her with your presence, but you double the intervals between your responses to teach her to stop crying for attention and that it's time to go to sleep. During the day, you will be there in abundance to give her the attention and love she needs.

How do you know when a child is crying for attention and not for some other reason? The answer is that you have to learn to distinguish between different types of cry and know your baby. Unusual cries should be responded to immediately – never ignore your child if she is crying like that, and waste no time investigating why.

Crying for attention or comfort has a different pattern. It often starts with a fretful, complaining sort of sound, or a sudden wail, but it breaks off while the child waits to see whether you will respond. Cry – pause – cry – pause – cry – it comes in waves, building toward a climax. It sounds a bit like the throttle or starter motor in a car revving up. You can hear anger and determination in the cry. Once you have learned how to distinguish this type of cry, you can try the technique:

★ When your child wakes in the night, listen to her cry. If you are sure that the cry is a cry for comfort or attention, wait a moment. Try to stay calm.

★ After she has cried for a short while, go to her. Don't pick her up. Soothe her with a comforting sound – no words – and gently rub her back for a little while. Don't make eye contact, which will stimulate her into full wakefulness. Keep the lights off. You are showing her that you are still at hand, that you haven't gone away, but that it's night-time now. Don't wait until she has dropped off to sleep again. When she is calm, leave the room.

★ A baby monitor is no substitute for seeing for yourself and improving your intuition.

★ The next time she cries, repeat the same stages, but wait for double the time before you go to her. If you waited two minutes the first time, wait four minutes this time. It doesn't matter if she started crying as soon as you left, or if it's an hour later. What you are trying to do is break a pattern.

★ Keep doubling the interval each time she wakes. It's tough at first, and I've known Moms to shed tears themselves when it all got a bit overwhelming. But you have to stick with it.

★ You may well find that your child will wake only half as many times the very next night, and that you have matters well under control within a week.

KEY POINT

Stick with it. Dealing with a crying baby is painful for parents. Make sure you don't tackle this technique on your own if you can help it. You'll need support from your partner, or a friend or relative. Remember that you are not neglecting your child; you are training her to get to sleep on her own.

Tip: Weaning
If you continue breastfeeding, or bottlefeeding, after your child is having three meals of solid food a day, don't feed him during the night or he will continue to wake up to seek the comfort of sucking. Feed him during the day by all means, and last thing at night, and first thing in the morning. But when he wakes at night, don't offer the breast or bottle.

Q. Will my lively toddler sleep better at night if I keep him awake all day? He's eighteen months old, and has a short nap in the morning and a longer one in the afternoon.

A. Keeping your son up all day won't make him sleep better at night. It's likely to have the reverse effect. By his normal bedtime, he will be so overtired and wound up, you may find that it's harder for him to get to sleep and stay asleep. Children who don't get enough sleep at night often wake up earlier, too. It's a vicious circle, no two ways about it.

At eighteen months, your son still needs a lot of sleep – on average about 13 hours, although some kids vary in their needs by a couple of hours each way. At some point around eighteen months, most toddlers can do without a morning nap. If he is only napping for a short time in the morning, it sounds like your son is ready for this change. But he will still need a nap in the afternoon if he's going to function well. It is unusual for the afternoon nap to disappear before the age of three. Even after this age, a child might drop off in the pushchair or in the car seat if he's had a busy morning or afternoon.

By all means, keep your toddler awake in the morning. He's at the age when he's ready to be stimulated by different sorts of activities – you might take him to a toddler group or club, for example. At the same time, bring his lunch forward and put him down for his afternoon nap earlier, say around 1:00 p.m. That way you will not run the risk of overtiring him.

You don't mention what problems you are having with him at night-time. If he's clingy, try the Sleep-Separation Technique (page 102). If he's crying and calling for you, try the Controlled-Crying Technique (page 90). If he's hard to put to bed in the first place, you may need to make some adjustments to your Bedtime Routine (page 88).

G is for Giving.
Be generous on every level in your parenting.

Q *My five-and-a-half-year-old daughter is scared of the dark. We've tried keeping her bedroom door open so she can see the light in the hall. We've put a nightlight in her room. But it's no use. She says there are monsters under her bed waiting to get her. We've both explained over and over that there are no such things as monsters, but she's still terrified. The worst thing is she won't go to the toilet when she needs to because she thinks they're under her bed, and she's having accidents nearly every night. Is this a phase, or will we ever get a decent night's sleep again?*

A I'm glad you made the connection between the bedwetting and the scary monsters. If something's on their mind, children of this age can start to wet the bed again after being dry at night for ages.

So first I would ask you to think about whether there are any stresses or tensions in the home that she might be picking up on. Small children sense very quickly if something's not quite right. She might not understand what's going on, but the "monsters" could be her way of expressing her feelings. Or she may simply be having nightmares. Does she go to sleep and then wake up scared? Or are the monsters part of an attention-seeking pattern? Whatever the reason, if you become very animated when you try to soothe her, she will learn to use this attention to her advantage and those monsters will stick around for a while.

What you have to do here is break the pattern. You and I know there are no scary monsters under her bed, or bogeymen hiding in the closet, but your daughter doesn't — and trying to tell her the monsters aren't there is not going to change her mind. What you have to do instead is jump into her world.

Try the **Magic-Dust Technique**. I used this on *Supernanny* to banish monsters from a little girl's bedroom who was about the same age as your daughter. Jasmine had a lot of problems with bedtime, and being frightened of monsters was one of them. The solution was to create an atmosphere where she felt safe.

So this is what you need:

- One pot of magic dust
- One fairy book or bedtime story
- One magic wand
- One superhero parent with bags of energy

You Dads out there, this a marvelous technique for you. Little kids — little girls especially — look up to their Dads as their protectors. But if Dad's not around, don't worry — Moms can be superheroes, too!

Basically, what you do is call on the help of some friendly fairies that you just happen to know to chase the monsters away. You need to be believable and speak like you really do know those invisible fairies. Don't be concerned that you might be reinforcing your child's belief in monsters. What you are doing is taking up her story, shifting it along, and giving it a proper ending. She will respond really well to the fact that you have come into her world, taken her fears seriously, and validated her feelings. You can use this technique for nightmares, too.

★ First, tell your daughter: "We're going to get rid of the monsters tonight. And the fairies are going to help us!"

★ Give your daughter a fairy book at bedtime and read her the story. This will give her a sense of security and make her feel protected.

★ Now it's time for a little acting. Wave the magic wand and say: "Monsters, monsters, go away!" Get her to join in with you.

★ Blow the glitter around the room. "Look, the fairies have dropped off some Magic Dust to help us!" Give it all you've got. Put the energy into being believable.

★ Chase the monsters out of the house – right out of the front door!

In Jasmine's case, this technique worked wonders, and she had her first dry night in three years. Her dad, Sunni, was brilliant in the role. His willingness to do what it took and his positive participation was what made the technique work so well.

Just to be on the safe side, you should combine it with the Elevenish-Get-Up-to-Pee Technique (page 104) in case other things are contributing to the bedwetting or it's becoming a bad habit. Leaving a potty in her room can help, too, especially if the loo's too far away to reach quickly. (And sometimes a child will make an extra effort to get to the bathroom rather than go back to using a potty.)

Q My seven-year-old son won't stay in bed. Every time we take him up to bed, he's back downstairs again within minutes. We've tried to explain to him that it's bedtime, but he just won't listen. It's got so bad lately we've given up trying and wait until he falls asleep on the sofa. I think part of the problem is the fact that his sister, who's twelve, is allowed to stay up later, and he doesn't want to be left out. But he's never been a very good sleeper.

A Waiting for your son to fall asleep on the sofa has got to stop. For a start, he needs to go to bed when you say so. Second, the situation you've got here is not fair to anyone. It's not fair to your daughter, who deserves some quality time with you and is old enough to stay up a bit later. And it's not fair to you as parents. You need time on your own, too. Most of all, it's not fair to your son, who can't be getting the rest he needs.

You need to address this problem in two ways. The first is to put a good bedtime routine into place if you haven't done so already. You say your son has never been a good sleeper. Some children find it harder to get to sleep than others, but at his age, he needs much more sleep than it sounds like he's getting, and he needs to learn how to get off to sleep by himself in his own bed. You can help him wind down at the end of the day by following a set routine (see page 88 for what to do).

Use this time for some one-to-one attention – make it a special time for him. That way he won't feel like he's missing out. Don't over-stimulate him or involve him in active play. Instead, read to him, talk to him, sing songs, have a cuddle – whatever makes the pair of you feel close. It's a good opportunity to have a chat about what happened during the day, and to talk about what's going to happen tomorrow. Take it in turns so that he gets special time with Mom and Dad. One night Mom puts him to bed; the next night Dad does.

After you put him to bed, use the **Stay-in-Bed Technique** to keep him where he should be. I've used this technique countless times and it always works if you follow it through, even in the toughest cases, where kids aren't just getting out of bed every two seconds, they're also screaming and throwing tantrums all over the place.

HOW THE TECHNIQUE WORKS

I usually recommend that the parent who has put the child to bed that night is the one who should take him back there when he gets up. This teaches the child that he cannot play one parent off against the other. But if he keeps getting out of bed time after time, there's no reason why you and your husband shouldn't take turns to take him back there, *provided* you are both capable of being strong. What you shouldn't do is call on your husband to help if you find yourself weakening – or vice versa. Both of you need to put the effort in and learn to stand your ground.

★ As soon as your child gets out of bed, take him back to bed and say: "It's bedtime, darling."

★ The next time he gets out of bed, take him back to bed and say: "Bedtime."

★ The third time he gets out of bed, take him back to bed and say *nothing*. Do not communicate with him at all and avoid eye contact as much as possible.

★ Every time he gets out of bed from then on, take him straight back to bed and say nothing.

★ The important thing is to persevere. It will work eventually. Sooner or later, he'll give up trying when he realizes there's no point. The first night you may be up and down the stairs twelve, thirteen, fourteen times. Some of the parents who write to me say that the first couple of nights it's taken them two hours to get their kids to stay in bed, but that the effort has been worth it, because they've seen a real improvement in a matter of days. When you're going up the stairs for the umpteenth time, remember that – and just think how toned you'll be after the workout. An advanced step-class is nothing in comparison!

KEY POINT

It sometimes takes parents a while to get the hang of this technique, especially if their child whines and pleads, or screams and shouts when he's being put back to bed. Even if he doesn't do those things, he may say he's thirsty, or hungry, or give a hundred and one different reasons why he needs to get out of bed.

Say it's the sixth time you're taking him back to bed. You're getting a bit fed up by now and have started to lose faith in the technique. Suddenly he announces: "I feel sick." What do you do?

All too often, parents are tempted to respond. "What do you mean, you feel sick? Have you got a temperature?"

"I've got a tummy ache," he says.

"You were all right a minute ago," you say. "Back to bed now." And you try to drag him up the stairs.

"I DON'T WANT TO GO TO BED!" he says at the top of his lungs.

Then, before you know it, you've lost it.

I know it's hard, especially if he's winding you up, but don't engage with him. Remember, the second time, all you say is: "Bedtime." *After that, say nothing.*

If he tells you he needs the bathroom or feels sick, respond without communicating. Take him to the bathroom without speaking to him, then take him back to bed when he's finished. Feel his forehead or take his temperature to see if he is running a fever when he says he's not feeling well. Use your body language to signal your determination to see the technique through.

I visited a family once where the little boy, Nathaniel, was using his diabetes as a get-out-of-jail-free card. "I'm having a hypo!" he would say, to justify not staying in bed. (A "hypo" is a serious fall in blood sugar levels, which can result in fainting or unconsciousness. It's a diabetic emergency.) When I introduced the Stay-in-Bed Technique to Nathaniel's Mom, it was hard for her not to respond to this kind of call for help. But she really rose to the occasion. The next time Nathaniel announced he was having a "hypo," instead of engaging with him, she collected his blood-testing kit, pricked his finger, waited for the result, and, when it proved to be normal, went downstairs again. Without saying a word. She was both decisive and responsible – she showed her son that she was not ignoring his condition, but that he could not use his illness to manipulate the situation.

H is for Humor. *See the light side of things!*

Q *Couldn't most sleep problems be avoided if you take your kids to bed with you? I've breastfed both my children in my bed and slept with them, too. It's always seemed a wonderful and natural way of being close. My four-year-old still comes into bed with us a few nights a week.*

A If that arrangement is causing you no problems and it works for your family, then good for you.

However, most of the parents who will read this answer and who have their children in bed with them night after night will have resorted to co-sleeping as a way of not tackling a sleep problem. They may not want their kids to be in bed with them at all. So "no" is the answer to your question: sleep problems can't be "avoided" this way. You have to take responsibility and deal with the problem, not avoid the issue.

Kids wind up in their parents' bed for lots of reasons – nightmares, separation anxiety, emotional immaturity, or simply to seek attention. There are a number of techniques you can use to deal with this situation, including the Sleep-Separation Technique (page 102) and the Stay-in-Bed Technique (page 96). What you won't find in this book is a Take-Your-Child-to-Bed-with-You Technique.

It's very important to teach children to initiate sleep by themselves and not be codependent on their parents. Co-sleeping often means that a child never learns how to go to sleep by herself properly, and will find it more difficult to separate from her parents than a child who has been encouraged to sleep in her own bed. From a very young age, all her experience of sleeping has been by your side. When you eventually decide you'd like your bed back, she simply won't have the resources to make the transition easily. Of course, it can be done and some children manage it by themselves. But there are lots of other ways to be close to your children without bringing them into your bed.

Even fans of the family bed accept that by the age of two or three, your child should be sleeping alone. In my experience, bed-sharing can go on much longer than that, by which time it will have begun to have an effect on your relationship as a couple. Privacy is important for parents. You need time and space to nurture your own relationship. As I said earlier, it's not just a question of a healthy sex life, although that's important, too. Couples need time to be alone and move their relationship on to the next stage. Parents who are with their kids 24/7 don't get the chance to do that, and what began as a loving partnership can quite easily turn stale.

Do not bring an infant into your bed; he could be smothered. Sharing a bed with your children can also pose a risk if you're a smoker, if you have been drinking, if you are overweight, or if you are very tired. And unless your bed is huge, the type of sleep you will be getting may be less than ideal. Partners can find it difficult enough to adjust to each other's sleeping habits – snoring, cover-hogging, tossing and turning. When there's three or four of you in the bed, someone's going to suffer.

Q *I've got two little girls who are six and three. They go to bed easily enough, but they don't stay there. Most mornings I wake up with either one or both of them in bed with me, without really knowing how (or when) they got there. My husband travels a lot on business and when he's away I don't really mind, but it's starting to become an issue between us when he's home. I don't see how I can put them back to bed when I don't even hear them come in. Should we get a bigger bed?*

A A bigger bed is NOT the answer! Your time together as a couple is precious enough as it is, especially since your husband is away from home a lot. You need as much time together as a couple as possible to keep your relationship going – and that includes child-free time in bed. It's not just a question of your sex life, though that's important, too. Marriages and adult partnerships need intimacy – privacy – to develop and grow.

You've got a double standard going on here. You don't mind the company of your kids when your husband's away. Then, when he returns, your girls are sent packing. I've seen the same thing happen with single parents. As long as the parent is single, the kids are welcome in their bed. Then, when a new relationship comes along, it's a different story. The kids are confused and jealous, and the new partner wonders what they've let themselves in for.

Your kids need a proper routine that addresses their needs, not yours. They need to be able to initiate sleep in their own beds and to take ownership of their own rooms so they are comfortable in their own space. At the same time, you need to face up to the feelings you have when your husband is away and learn to sleep on your own. Are you taking your kids to bed with you to avoid addressing their sleep problems? Or yours?

When one parent has sole care of the kids for long periods of time, it can be tempting to relax and let the kids get away with things that they wouldn't be allowed to do if the other parent was there to help enforce the rules. This sends out a mixed message. Your kids will be thinking: "Is it OK to get into Mom and Dad's bed, or not?" Or they might start to play you off against each other. With Dad away for long periods, you need to keep to a consistent approach more than ever. This will help Dad get back in his groove when he returns home. If you are lax while he is away, and he comes back and suddenly the rules are being enforced again, your kids won't look forward to his return as much as they should. Why should they? They're living the life of Riley while Dad's away and now that he's back, they've got to mind their Ps and Qs.

When you're on your own with your kids, it's tempting to treat them more as friends than children who are dependent on you. You may think this makes it easier and avoids conflict, but a child who's being encouraged to see her Mom as a friend first and a parent second will be confused and insecure. She needs to look to you for guidance and boundaries, not be awarded equal status when she doesn't have the first idea how to handle such a role and isn't equipped to deal with it. Letting your child sleep in your bed can give her the impression that you are both on the same footing, that you are buddies or pals, not mother and daughter.

I can fully understand why you might not mind having your kids in bed with you when your husband is away. You're virtually a single parent for a lot of the time, and the job can be tiring and lonely. Another body in bed – even a small wriggling one – can be comforting. But you should be looking for comfort in other ways.

One of the things you should be thinking about is whether *you* are getting the support you need. See if you can arrange to go out once in a while or have a friend over for supper. Adult company can help you put things in perspective and maintain your role as your daughters' Mom, not their friend. Ask a friend or relative to babysit for your children, so you can have some "Me" time. Try to encourage your husband to spend quality time with your girls when he comes home. If he gets back late on a Friday evening, make the girls rest for a while in the afternoon so they can stay up later and see their Dad. Take time out to rest yourself and have a break from the single-parent role. Falling into bed exhausted night after night will take its toll – and it might be the reason why you don't wake up easily when your kids come into your bedroom.

How can you tell when your kids have crept into bed with you? Use the Chimes Technique:

HOW THE TECHNIQUE WORKS

★ Hang wind chimes on your bedroom door, or a string of bells, or anything else that makes a noise loud enough to wake you up.

★ As soon as the chimes ring, telling you that your bed is about to be invaded, take your kids straight back to their own beds. Don't be tempted to turn over and go back to sleep. It may take a few nights before they get the message, but it is important to follow through each time.

★ If your kids won't stay in bed after you've taken them back there, use the Stay-in-Bed Technique (page 96).

★ Remember that you can always have cuddles with your kids in bed on weekend mornings. And you can always bring them into your bed when they are ill and need special attention.

Tip: Using the technique
The Chimes Technique is good for alerting you to any kind of night-time disturbance – for example, if your child is coming to tell you she has wet the bed or had a bad dream.

H is for Honesty.
Honesty is the only foundation on which to build trust.

Q Ever since we moved our two-year-old son from a crib into a "big bed," he won't go to sleep unless one of us is lying down beside him. It seems to take longer and longer every night for him to get to sleep. Once my husband fell asleep before my son did! What are we doing wrong? Should we move him back into his crib for a while?

A I get loads of letters from parents saying that now their child can climb out of his crib, does this mean he should be in a big bed? Toddlers do become more agile as their physical skills and strength develop, and it is not surprising that they learn how to mountaineer over the sides of their cribs. That's not always enough reason to move a child to a big bed. Lower the crib sides so he doesn't hurt himself and practice the Sleep-Separation Technique opposite to keep him where he belongs at night.

Unless a child has outgrown the crib altogether, I wouldn't recommend a move into a "big bed" before the age of three. Three is a much more mature age when a child can be involved in the whole process. You can talk things over with a three-year-old, prepare him for the change, and even take him to the shop to choose his bed. At two, the change might seem more sudden and unsettling.

If your son was getting to sleep with no problems before the move into his "big bed," the transition could well be bothering him. Now that you've made the move, however, it's not a good idea to retrace your steps and put him back into the crib. You may well create more problems than you solve. The answer is to get him used to going to sleep without depending on your being there. Once a pattern of dependency is established, for whatever reason, children quickly learn to use it as a means of control, as you are beginning to find out!

Try the **Sleep-Separation Technique** below, or the Stay-in-Bed Technique (page 96), depending on his emotional maturity. The Sleep-Separation Technique gradually removes your presence from your son's bedroom so he can get to sleep on his own.

HOW THE TECHNIQUE WORKS

★ Put your son to bed in the usual way, give him a cuddle, and tell him to close his eyes and that it's time to go to sleep. Make sure that the light is off and the door is open.

★ Sit down on the floor close to the bed, but at arm's length, so he can't reach for you. Don't look at him. Just sit in silence until he goes to sleep. Every time he tries to talk to you, say nothing. Body language is key. Sit with your head down, like you were shut off. You're reassuring him with your presence, but not engaging with him in any other way.

★ He will try to involve you in a conversation, or ask for a story, a drink of water, or any other delaying tactic he might think of. So make sure you've ticked all the boxes before you start the technique. Give him a sip of water, read him a story, and follow the bedtime routine as normal.

Tip: Ease the transition
Ease the transition to a big bed by putting your child's favorite toys on it. Make the bed with his favorite blanket – anything that shows him that it's his territory.

★ The next night, repeat the same stages, moving a little way farther from the bed.

★ Gradually increase the distance between you and the bed until you are sitting outside his room with the door open. In your son's case, it probably won't take too long to break the cycle, particularly as he was getting to sleep on his own when he was in his crib. When the pattern has been going on for some time, it takes longer to break it.

Q *About four months ago, my five-year-old son started wetting the bed again, after being dry at night since he was three and a half. It started with just a couple of accidents once in a while, but now he wets the bed every night, sometimes two or three times. We've been using a star chart to reward him for dry nights – but these are few and far between! Of course, he wakes up every time he wets the bed, and then I have to change the sheets, so none of us are getting much sleep.*

A It is important to try to find out what is behind the bedwetting. Most kids continue to have the odd accident after they are dry at night, but it's usually easy to work out why – they've had more to drink before bedtime than normal, they're in a strange bed, there's been some disruption to their routine, or they went to bed overexcited… Many children also lose bladder control temporarily when they're ill. But these are usually one-offs. What you've got here is a pattern developing.

The first step is to make sure the bedwetting does not have a physical cause, such as candida, diabetes, or a urinary infection. Take your son to your GP and have his urine tested.

If he's not suffering from an infection, think back over the last four months and try to pinpoint any changes or events that might have upset him. Moving to a new house, starting school, the arrival of a new baby sister or brother, and other family upsets can trigger a spell of bedwetting. If older kids are not given a good introduction to a new sibling, for example, they can regress in their behavior to get attention again.

I met a woman recently at a conference who asked me what she should do about her four-year-old son. He'd been dry for a year, but had just started to wet the bed again and it was really upsetting her. I ran through the points I've just outlined above. Any medical problems? No. Too much to drink late at night? No. Any upheavals in his life recently? No. "Are you sure?" I said. "Think back over the past few months. Could anything be stressing him?" "No," she said. "But *I've* been pretty stressed. I had another baby four months ago and we've just moved to a new house!"

Kids are part of your life, too. Your stresses and strains are going to impact on them.

Bedwetting can also go along with a fear of the dark (page 89). Sometimes, however, it's just about attention-seeking.

In the meantime, what should you do about it?

★ Restrict your child's fluid intake in the last hours before bed.

★ Make sure that he has a pee before he goes to bed.

★ Buy a few extra sheets (get some cheap ones from a discount store) and put a waterproof undersheet on the bed to protect the mattress.

* You can also buy an alarm pad to place under the sheets. A bell will go off when he wets the bed, which will help to alert you. Or you can hang wind chimes or bells from your bedroom door so that you wake up when he comes in to tell you what's happened (page 101).

* Use the **Elevenish-Get-Up-to-Pee Technique**. Until he can make it through the night again, you will have to wake him up about 11:00 p.m. and take him to the toilet. It is important that you wake him up enough so that he is aware of what is happening – what you are trying to do is encourage him to get up and pee by himself when he needs to.

* Stay supportive and calm. When he wets the bed, say: "Oh dear. You wet the bed tonight, but maybe you'll have a dry night tomorrow."

* And keep going with the star chart. With luck, he'll have some stars on it soon.

I'm glad to hear that you're changing the sheets. Never make a child sleep in a wet bed as a punishment – a bedwetting child needs support, not punishment. Some parents get so fed up being woken in the middle of the night that they make their anger clear. Scolding only makes bedwetting children feel worse. They're ashamed enough of themselves as it is. Shame can even make a child stay in a wet bed rather than tell you what's happened.

It can also be tempting, faced with night after night of broken sleep, to put the child back in diapers or pull-ups for a while. This is also very upsetting for the child – it's a big step backwards and will make him feel like a big baby. Encourage his sense of independence. If he's five or six, you can get him to help you make the bed. Praise and encourage him for trying.

I is for Involvement.
Get your kids involved in what you do. Togetherness strengthens the family unit.

Q *I really miss sleeping in on the weekend with my partner. We've got two children, a girl of six and a boy who's three and a half, and they both get up at seven. Is there any way of making them sleep in a little longer on weekends? They both sleep through the night and we've never had many problems settling them down – it's just that we'd like our sleep-ins back!*

A Hello! Your kids sleep through the night and get up at seven. Some kids get up at 5:30 a.m.! If you have managed to avoid any sleep problems with your children so far, you're doing really well. So the first thing I would say is: "If it ain't broke, why fix it?"

Even if you kept your kids up a bit later the previous night, at their ages they probably wouldn't sleep any longer the next morning. Instead, you would run the risk of depriving them of sleep that they need and making them more irritable the next day. It's only when children are older that you can afford to keep them up a bit longer so they sleep in later the next morning. Even so, I'm talking an hour or so, not an adult's idea of a sleep-in. Children can't switch from one routine to another at the drop of a hat just because it's the weekend. You've got a sleep pattern going with your kids that many parents would give their eyeteeth for – be grateful for that!

As parents, you can't expect life to go on as it did before your kids came along. You have to accept that long mornings in bed are a thing of the past for the time being. If you both need more sleep to recharge your batteries on weekends, take turns getting up with the kids. Otherwise, take advantage of the fact that your nights are trouble-free to enjoy time together as a couple in the evening. If you tailor your own sleep pattern so that you go to bed earlier, you will wake up feeling more refreshed and won't need the extra sleep.

You might be able to win yourself another half-hour in bed by explaining to your children that you'll be up in a short while and in the meantime they can play quietly in their bedroom. If you put on a children's video for them to watch, it's not the worst thing in the world from time to time.

Otherwise, I would suggest you bring your kids into bed with you on weekend mornings with a few toys and books. It's a great time for families to snuggle up and be close.

I is for Inner Child.
Step into your child's world and release your inner child.

4 Home and Away

Behavioral issues aren't just confined to eating and sleeping. In my work on *Supernanny,* I often see parents struggling across the board with a whole range of difficulties, both within the home and outside it. And if the hundreds of letters and emails I receive from worried Moms and Dads are anything to go by, these concerns are shared by a lot of people around the world.

How do you stop kids from running out of the house?
How do you get them to behave in social situations?
How do you do the weekly shopping without your kids having a screaming fit in the supermarket?
What about swearing? Whining? Lying?
Or the child who's too shy to say "hello"?

Parenting throws up a lot of challenges – and many gray areas. A child who is intimidating and consistently aggressive, who kicks, hits, and fights, clearly needs to have his behavior curbed. But what about the child who can't get herself ready in time for school? Or the three-year-old who's not potty-trained yet? Part of parenting consists of caring for a child's physical needs. Making sure he has enough sleep, the right food to eat, nursing him when he's ill, keeping him warm, dry, clothed, and giving him the opportunity to run around in the fresh air are all part of the job description. But as a parent you are not simply a caregiver, your role is to nurture emotional needs, too. Raising your kids – the next generation – means listening to them and guiding them so

they can gain an understanding of others. It means teaching them the social skills they need to get on with other people and encouraging them to be more independent, confident, and self-reliant; to grow up to be well-rounded, happy individuals in their own right.

Household rules set boundaries in place. Kids who are not given any boundaries by their parents are put in the position of being in charge of their own upbringing. You might think that letting kids rule the roost – letting them do what they want – would be guaranteed to make them happy. The reverse is true. Kids who don't have any limits imposed on their behavior are far from carefree. Instead, they are often confused, which makes them frightened and insecure. If they get away with everything, this tells them they're in charge and that this must be the way you want them to continue to behave. They don't want that freedom or that responsibility. From a young age, they need direction and guidance.

Sometimes parents allow children to go undisciplined because they think that any form of control whatsoever will crush the child's spirit or spoil the relationship they have with their child. Or they may have been brought up in a strict household, and are determined to give their children a completely free rein to express their feelings without any form of discipline. At the other extreme are parents who pay no attention to their kids' emotional needs at all and expect them to stick to the straight and narrow. What I try to do is to bring the two sides together and give kids a framework

in which they can explore safely and learn to think for themselves, as well as teach them the social skills that will enable them to get on with other people.

There are also parents who are unwilling to discipline their kids or set boundaries for their behavior in case they get it wrong. I see this a lot. The parents disapprove of the way their kids are behaving – but they just won't step up to the plate and take responsibility. They may lack confidence in their parenting skills, or think someone's going to point a finger and label them bad parents or say they're inadequate in some way. So instead of engaging with the issues they need to deal with, they take a back seat or resort to short-term diversions, worried about being judged.

Find the courage to give it what it takes. Show your kids where the boundaries are by setting them. Lead by example, so your kids have models for their behavior. I've never visited a family where love was in short supply. But I've seen plenty where respect had gone right out of the window. Setting boundaries and keeping them in place with discipline *and* praise and encouragement creates a healthy family life where there's love and respect on all sides. It's all about balance.

Topics and techniques covered in this chapter:

HOUSEHOLD RULES and how to set boundaries in place

SEPARATION ANXIETY and how to deal with it

SEPARATION TECHNIQUE for happy good-byes

TIMER TECHNIQUE to teach kids to share

SHARING BINS to teach siblings to share

SIBLING RIVALRY and how to deal with it

ANGER MANAGEMENT using breathing and exercise

SHYNESS – how to give your kids social skills

WHINING and how to deal with it

TOILET-TRAINING do's and don'ts

BIG-BOY/BIG-GIRL TECHNIQUE to teach toddlers to dress themselves

FADDY DRESSING and how to deal with it

BATHTIME BLUES and how to deal with it

RISE-AND-SHINE TECHNIQUE/GET-UP-AND-GO CHART for stress-free mornings

TRUST TECHNIQUE for kids who stay out too late

ROAMING TECHNIQUE for kids who run off

BAD BEHAVIOR IN PUBLIC and how to deal with it

THE INVOLVEMENT TECHNIQUE for supermarket shopping

CAR TRIPS – coping strategies

SETTLING YOUR CHILD AT A NURSERY OR SCHOOL

BACKTALK and how to deal with it

TELLING LIES and how to deal with it

HOMEWORK and how to support your child

CHORES and how to get your kids involved

J is for Journey.

Parenting is a journey. Recognize the milestones you achieve along the way and the adversities you overcome.

Household rules

Some of the families I work with already have a clear idea which household rules they would like to implement, it's just that they're having trouble enforcing them. In other families, Mom and Dad don't agree what the rules are, or change them, moving the goalposts as soon as their kids' behavior becomes too challenging. Kids grow up – families evolve. It's very rare for parents to have no rules at all. Almost every parent, for example, is going to find aggressive behavior – hitting, punching, kicking – unacceptable. But the way they deal with these issues often tells their kids a different story.

A rule is only a rule if you back it up with a consequence if it's broken. If you don't communicate how you expect your kids to behave, and steer them in the right direction with a combination of discipline and praise, you might as well have no rules at all. As adults, we accept that we are governed by certain rules in society. We know that if we go through a red light and get caught, we're going to get a ticket. Kids need to understand that their behavior, good and bad, has consequences.

Imagine sitting down to play a board game with your child. You've played the game before, but she hasn't. You set it up and tell your child she can go first. "What do I do?" she asks. But you don't tell her. "Do I roll the dice?" she asks. You say nothing. So she rolls the dice and moves her piece along the board. "You're going the wrong way," you say. "How am I supposed to know?" asks your daughter. "You didn't tell me!"

One of the first things I do on *Supernanny*, after I've had time to assess the family

dynamic and spoken to the parents, is to sit the family down and give them a household routine. At the same time, if there's inconsistency about household rules or the family needs reminding what they are, I write them down on a large sheet of paper and stick the paper on the wall, on the fridge, or some other place where everyone can see it. I'm not talking about pages and pages of rules that cover every single aspect of family life down to the last detail; I'm talking about a basic framework. Often the rules will highlight certain kinds of behavior that are a particular problem in that household – swearing, for example, or fighting.

Go back to the example of the board game. You're not going to sit down with your three-year-old and teach her how to play Monopoly. She just wouldn't have the mental skills to understand all the rules and know what she has to do. At her age, throwing the dice, taking turns, and moving from square to square on the board is enough to deal with. She's at the Chutes and Ladders stage. The same is true of household rules. Small children need a few clear rules: "No fighting." "Do what Mommy and Daddy say." As your children get older, you can move on and fine-tune their behavior to a greater degree.

What you're aiming for is to get your kids to the point where they are more consciously aware of their behavior and other people, and have a sense within themselves of what's right and wrong. When a child has developed her own conscience, she will come to you with an apology when she has done something she knows is wrong without being asked.

Now you don't have to write down your household rules and pin them up on the wall. But you may well have to pick a quiet moment with your partner to discuss ways in which you can find a common approach. What's unacceptable behavior? What's OK? Which issues do you as parents really need to get on top of? Which areas can you afford to be more relaxed about? Use the Same-Page Technique (page 30) to sort out any differences so you present a united front. Communicate with one another, and with your children.

Make it clear how you want your children to behave, and why, when you leave them in the care of nannies, baby-sitters, au pairs, and mother's helpers. As much as possible, everyone who looks after your kids should stick to the same basic agenda so your kids know what's expected.

Having a clear set of household rules doesn't mean you've got to spend every day with a policeman's hat on, bringing your kids up short left, right, and center. Don't go looking for trouble. Praise and encouragement – validating how well your kids are doing – are just as powerful as discipline when it comes to getting your kids to behave. But it's also important to realize that you will fight fewer battles if you nip bad behavior in the bud before it gets a chance to escalate. Many parents ignore backtalk or relatively minor misdemeanors for the sake of a quiet life, hoping it will all blow over. But if the bad behavior is very ingrained, or if the child is misbehaving for attention, she's going to up the ante. And before long, you'll be picking up the pieces

after a major outburst. If she breaks a rule, you must warn her and follow through as soon as the behavior is repeated.

When I first visited Wendy Agate, a single mom with three school-age daughters, she was at a very low ebb. As far as her kids' behavior was concerned, she had thrown in the towel. There was next to no respect in that house, and the youngest daughter, seven-year-old Mary-Ann, was virtually out of control. Mom had been struggling for four years since her partner left and had very low self-esteem. Her relationship with her daughter had started to follow the same negative pattern she had had with her former partner. It took time to build up Wendy's confidence so she could communicate her authority as a parent and stop letting rip at her kids out of anger and frustration. One of the things I noticed was that Wendy found it hard to follow through. One breakfast time, a power struggle developed between her and Mary-Ann over a piece of toast. Wendy let it pass, and the next thing she knew she had a full-blown tantrum to deal with. In many ways, Mary-Ann was testing her mother to see if she would step up and take on the parental role. During the time I worked with her, Wendy came a long way. By the time I left, Wendy was proud to have finally got hold of the title "Mom," and was not going to let it slip away again.

Here are some points to think about:

★ **BE CONSISTENT AS PARENTS** about what you allow and don't allow. Inconsistency confuses kids and gives them the perfect opportunity to play one parent off against the other. "But Mom says it's OK!"

★ **DON'T BE PETTY** Set clear rules about the big stuff, but don't waste time trying to enforce loads and loads of minor rules about the finer points of conduct. There's a fine line between controlling the child and controlling the situation.

★ **LEAD BY EXAMPLE** You can't expect your kids to take notice of what you say unless you behave the same way, too. Swearing is a classic example. If the air turns blue every time you open your mouth, you can expect your kids to pick up that vocabulary in no time flat. If it's a "bad word," why are you using it?

★ **BACK UP YOUR RULES WITH DISCIPLINE** It isn't a rule if you don't enforce it.

★ **PRAISE AND ENCOURAGEMENT** go a long way, especially when you see kids behave well without any initiation or direction on your part.

KEY POINT

Offering choices is no substitute for having a clear set of rules. I'm constantly seeing parents offering too many choices to small children to get them to cooperate and behave. "You don't want that?" "No?" "Well how about this then?" "No?" On and on and on. Small children can't cope with loads of choices, any more than they can cope with being in charge. To them the issue may have nothing to do with dressing, eating, playing, or whatever activity they're engaged in at the time. It's simply about control. Limit the choices you offer them, try to involve them in what you're doing, and back up your rules with discipline if necessary.

Tip: Because
Always explain the rules to your kids. Your four-year-old is about to leave the table with her mouth full. You tell her not to. She says: "Why?" Don't just say: "Because." Tell her: "It's good manners to sit at the table until you've finished. Then you may ask to be excused."

K is for Kindness.
Show your kids compassion and basic human kindness.

Q My son Ben, who's thirteen months old, is really clingy. He cries when I leave the room and won't go to his Dad at all. He won't engage with his toys, and wants to sit on my lap all the time.

A Provided your son is not ill or under any emotional stress, what he's probably experiencing is separation anxiety. Your child is old enough to remember and compare events, so when he sees you leaving, he gets upset because he remembers he didn't like it the last time you went. Sticking like glue to Mom is another feature of separation anxiety and can make Dads feel left out in the cold.

How does his wailing make you feel? It's not unusual for Moms to feel trapped and overwhelmed when they can't even go for a pee without their child getting upset. Stay calm, take a deep breath, and keep talking to your son in an everyday voice to show him he has nothing to worry about. Don't let him transfer his anxiety to you. A baby just needs to hear your voice when you step into the next room. For a toddler, keeping up a running commentary is sometimes enough to reassure him. What you shouldn't do is tiptoe out of the room when he's not looking – as soon as he notices you've gone, that will only confirm his worst fears.

I like to play peekaboo games with small children to teach them that what they can't see is still there. Try pulling a muslin cloth or tea towel over your head and reappearing all of a sudden – it's bound to make him laugh. Or roll yourself up in the covers. Hiding balls or objects under cups is another fun game.

Reassure your partner that his son has not taken an instant dislike to him. The intensity of this phase will pass, especially if you don't over-react. If you pacify your son when you hand him over to his Dad – "It's all right, darling, oh, I know you're upset" – you're validating what he's feeling and you don't want to do that.

But be warned: Separation anxiety tends to come back again around the age of eighteen months. Prepare for that time by widening his social world so he becomes more confident around different people.

L *is for Love.*
Love is unconditional. It's the strongest force there is.

Q *Help! We have no social life at all. Our three-year-old daughter gets so upset if we go out for the evening that we've given up trying.*

A lot of parents face this problem – and some react the same way you have, by abandoning any attempt to have a social life. First of all, you've both got to remind yourselves that quality time together as a couple *outside the home* is important to keep your relationship going. Being a parent is not about putting your needs on hold for eighteen years.

Small children often put on Academy Award–winning performances at the front door when they know their parents are going out for the evening. It doesn't mean you have to add to the drama. Some children find it harder to separate from their parents than others, but most will go through a period of clinginess when they are reluctant to be cared for by anyone else.

Here are ways to cope with the situation (staying in isn't one of them!):

★ Make sure that you use a sitter whom your daughter knows and trusts. It could be Grandma (if she's willing) or a family member. Otherwise, invite the sitter to come over and get to know your daughter during the day when you can reassure her with your presence. Don't leave her with someone she doesn't know. That will compound the problem.

★ Reserve a table at a restaurant or buy cinema tickets and book the sitter for the evening in question.

★ Timing is key. It might help if you ask the sitter to come early so that your daughter can get settled in a game or activity before you leave the house. But if your daughter has worked out the equation – baby-sitter comes in the door = parents leaving – she might well act up as soon as the sitter arrives. In this case, you should make sure you don't delay your departure.

★ Don't try to sneak out the door. When it's time to leave, explain to your daughter that you're going out and that you'll be back later on. Keep it short and sweet. Give her a kiss and a cuddle. Don't validate her feelings by pacifying her and telling her that you know she's going to be upset.

★ Leave confidently and enjoy your evening. In most cases, the tears will be dry before you're out of sight of the house. By all means take your cell phone with you, but resist the temptation to call every five minutes to check how she is. Ask yourself – are you a parent who likes her dependency?

For children who find it hard to let their parents go, I use the Separation Technique – a summary of how it works is on the next page.

In one of the families I worked with, the Harmonys, Mom had fallen into the trap of pacifying the behavior of her three-year-old son. Whenever she tried to leave the house, Grant would chase the car down the driveway like he was training for the 100-meter sprint. She'd stop the car, give him a kiss and a cuddle – and then the chase would start all over again. I used the **Separation Technique** to break Grant's grip on the apron strings.

HOW THE TECHNIQUE WORKS

★ Get yourself ready.

★ Give your sitter, partner, or whoever is looking after your child advance warning five minutes before you need to leave the house so they can set up an activity with your child.

★ Just before you go, explain in a confident way where you are going and what you will be doing. "Mom's going to run an errand. I'll be back in twenty minutes."

★ Say "Bye-bye" and leave.

Q *My four-year-old son has a real problem with sharing. Once he's got hold of a toy, he just won't let anyone else have a turn. It's bad enough when we're at someone else's house, but it's even worse at home. He really hates other children touching any of his toys. Please help with this problem because it's getting to the point where I'm reluctant to ask any of my friends to come over with their kids.*

A Toys are very important to children, and they can often be very territorial about them, especially in their own home. You're not the only parent with this problem. Four-year-olds like to be King of the Castle.

In the Doyle family, the kids found it so difficult to play nicely with others that Mom had stopped having people over because she was so embarrassed. She was virtually held ransom in her own home. I told the kids they were allowed to put one favorite toy away in their bedrooms, but they had to share the rest.

Teach your son that sharing can be fun. It doesn't mean that he has to give up his toys forever. Try the **Timer Technique**.

HOW THE TECHNIQUE WORKS

★ Get an egg timer and explain to your son that he can play with his toy until the timer runs out and then he must let his friends play with it. Tell him that once everyone has had a turn, he can have the toy back.

★ Once the time is up, encourage your son to hand the toy to another child. Don't attempt to take it from him – that will only turn into a tug-of-war. Instead, tell him that the time is up and he should hand the toy over to his friend for a little while. Praise him when he does. Every time he shares a toy, tell him how good he is and how happy he is making you.

★ Carry on with the timer, handing the toy to each child in turn, until it's your son's turn again.

★ You have to persevere. Eventually he will understand that sharing is a good thing to do, and doesn't mean a toy is gone forever.

★ You can also introduce games that mean he has to play with others, such as playing with a train set, playing in the sandpit, or water games. Try the Shared-Play Technique (page 219). When you are supervising the game – or playing it alongside the kids – be very animated and excited. This helps to communicate that sharing and taking turns leads to lots of fun.

Q *My three daughters are always fighting over their toys. At five, three, and two, they're pretty close in age, and this doesn't help. But I'm getting sick of refereeing the fights. They're pretty well-behaved otherwise. It's just the constant bickering and squabbling that is getting me down.*

A Sounds like a proper catfight! I think there are two issues you need to address here. You don't say what form the fights take, but if there's aggressive behavior, you need to put some discipline in place to make it clear that fighting is unacceptable to you. Establish house rules, so children will know what's acceptable. Use the Naughty Step or one of its variations (page 172). If the girls are all squabbling together, you can use separate Naughty Beanbags, Chairs, Spots, or Mats to teach them to cool down and stop fighting amongst themselves.

At the same time, what you also need to do is to teach them to share. Try the Shared-Play Technique (page 219). Or you can set them up with one of the activities outlined in the chapter Positive Feedback (page 198) that calls for cooperation – a treasure hunt, an obstacle course, water play – anything that gets them working as a team and having fun without focusing on their possessions.

I've also used a technique called **Sharing Bins** for a family whose kids were always fighting over who got to play with what.

HOW THE TECHNIQUE WORKS

✴ Get yourself a number of bins or containers – or even cardboard boxes. Give each girl a container and label it with her name.

✴ Lay out all your kids' toys on the floor.

✴ Go through the toys and help your daughters decide which toy belongs to which girl. Each girl should put her own toys in the container with her name on it.

✴ After all the toys have been separated into the three bins, ask each of your daughters to choose one toy from her bin that she will share with one of her sisters for a week.

✴ After they have successfully shared a few toys amongst themselves for a week, sit down with them again and give them another container. Label it SHARING BIN. Then ask your daughters to pick a few toys that can go into the Sharing Bin. Explain that these are the toys that belong to all of them.

M *is for Manners.*
Teach composure and good conduct, and lead by example so your kids learn to respect themselves and others.

Q *I've got a bad case of sibling rivalry on my hands. Adam, my oldest boy, is five, and ever since his little brother Toby was born six months ago, he's made it clear that he's very jealous of him, because his behavior has become more extreme. He's very aggressive around Toby – me, too, for that matter. He's just so angry all the time – it's like he's going to explode! What do we do?*

A First, you've got to find some compassion for what your son's going through. He's had you both to himself for nearly five years, the be-all and end-all of your world. Now a new baby has come along and everything's changed. It's not always as easy for a child to accept a new dynamic as it is for an adult.

The new baby has shaken Adam's equilibrium, and the aggression is his reaction to change. What you need to do is to work on getting him back on track by structuring your routine in such a way that it makes him feel equal. Give him time on a one-to-one basis and get him involved with what you're doing. Once he feels there's a secure structure in place that includes him, he should start to settle down.

Parents often rush to discipline their kids in this kind of situation. This only heightens their children's sense of injustice. However, if Adam carries on using his aggression after you've given him positive attention, I would use a Chill-Out Chair. When Adam acts aggressively, warn him that if he repeats the behavior, he will have to sit on the Chill-Out Chair for five minutes, think about his behavior, and get ready to apologize. See page 191 for how to implement the technique. The early stages of implementing any discipline technique are always very challenging, but it's important that you follow through every time.

Tip: Anger management
I would also teach your son how to deal with his anger before he gets a chance to erupt. Get him to practice breathing out all the hot air. Tell him to take a deep breath and then exhale slowly on a count of five. Or you could show him how to defuse his anger and tension by shaking out his arms and legs.

N is for Nurturing.
Nurture your children's emotional needs.

Q My oldest daughter, Sian, who's nine, is a really outgoing girl. But the younger one, Sophie, who's coming up on seven, is completely the opposite. She's very shy with just about everyone. She also whines a lot, which gets on my nerves. Why can't she be more like her sister? We treat her in exactly the same way.

A Hey. You've got two different kids here. Every child in every family is an individual. You can't expect them to be the same. Parenting is about working with what you've got – recognizing each child's unique temperament and personality, and adjusting your parenting style to suit so that you support the positive behavior. Of course, it's important to be consistent. I'm not suggesting that you have a different set of rules for each child. But kids can be raised in the same way, and given the same values, while you adjust the style of your approach according to their different personalities.

It's clear from your letter that you're holding up Sian as some sort of role model you expect Sophie to follow. And if it's clear to me, it's bound to be more than clear to Sophie, who may well be jealous of all the approval that her sister is getting for her confident behavior. Is she really shy? Or has shyness become her way of staking a claim for herself and getting some attention? What is the dynamic like between the two girls? Is Sophie always overshadowed by her sister? Does she find it difficult to get heard? She needs the emotional space to flourish in her own right without being constantly compared to her sister. With some kids,

shyness can also be a cover-up for laziness. Is Sophie letting her older sister speak for her?

Make sure you spend one-on-one time with both girls. Get Sophie involved with what you do to give her more confidence and independence. Have special times with her – a shopping trip, an outing, a social occasion. Make time for her to have her own friends over when Sian is out of the house so she can learn how to be more socially adept.

Some kids are naturally less outgoing than others: It's not a *character flaw*. But extreme shyness can be attention-seeking. Don't make a fuss over her shyness or give her more attention when she displays that kind of behavior around other people.

Are you expecting too much from Sophie? In the case of the Minyons, one of the families I visited on *Supernanny*, the two children, Frank and Skyler, refused to greet friends and family who came to the house or to initiate conversations with them. This caused huge embarrassment for their parents, who didn't see that the over-friendly behavior they expected of their kids was uncomfortable for them. Adults don't hug and kiss people they hardly know. Why should we expect kids to?

I drew four concentric chalk circles on the patio to demonstrate the different levels of personal space and show Mom and Dad that they were putting too much pressure on their kids in social situations. The four circles stood for four types of greeting: Wave, Handshake, Hugs, and Kisses. When I asked Dad to sit down in the inner circle and then stood over him, he could see how intimidated his kids might feel with a large adult looming over them, expecting a hug and kiss. Four-year-old Skyler was using her behavior as a form of attention-seeking, so I also worked with her using dolls to role-play the different ways people say hello and good-bye, and we went on to practice this together at the front door. Individual attention for both kids from both parents helped them to build up their confidence and open the doors of communication. Eventually, I encouraged the parents to take a back seat when guests came to the house, so that the kids could greet the arrivals on their terms without feeling pressured.

As far as the whining is concerned, of course it's going to get on your nerves. That's what it's designed to do. There are two kinds of whining. The first one is the persistent drip, drip, drip that's supposed to wear you down: "Please, please, please, please, *pretty please . . .*" The way you deal with this is to say: "Stop asking me."

The second kind of whining is when a child asks for things in a whiny, indistinct voice only bats could hear. "Wan ree," she says into her left shoulder. "What did you say?" "Wanna reenk." "Oh, you want a *drink*!"

When Sophie whines, don't give in to it (unless, of course, she's ill). Copy her whining tone of voice. Kids often collapse in giggles if you play their behavior back to them in an animated way. Tell her to speak to you in a normal tone of voice. Explain that you can't understand what she says when she whines. If she's asking for something that she's allowed to have, tell her she can have it when she asks properly.

O is for One-to-One.
One-on-one attention bonds the ties between each member of the family unit.

Q *How early can I start to toilet-train my daughter? She's nineteen months.*

A Toilet-training can't be forced. It's not up to a parent to decide the time frame. You've got to look out for the signs when your child is ready.

Trying to toilet-train a child before she's really ready is a mistake. Some parents are obsessed with getting their kids out of diapers as soon as possible. If you start too early, you're facing a long, uphill struggle. But if you get the timing right, you can toilet-train a child in a week, two at the max. In most cases, that's going to be when the child is between two and three years old. I would say that you probably have a good while to go before you can begin.

Until a child is eighteen months old, she won't yet have reached the physical stage of development that will allow her to control her bladder and bowels. A little later, around the age of two, and she will begin to take notice of those times when she goes. She may even announce she's having a pee or poo, or tell you after it's happened. Before you can start toilet-training, she has to be at the stage when she can communicate with you to some degree, so you can teach her how to spot the signs that she needs to go, and she can understand you when you prompt and encourage her. You might be able to spot the signs from her facial expressions or posture much earlier, but for toilet-training to succeed, she needs to be able to tell you verbally when she needs to go.

How can you tell when the right time is approaching? One way is to examine her diapers. If she's getting to the stage where she's dry and clean after a nap, she's nearing the point of voluntary control.

As I say, I think you're some way off this stage yet. But there are other ways you can start preparing your daughter to ensure that toilet-training goes as smoothly as possible when it is time to begin the process. Let her see *you* go to the toilet. Explain what's happening. Show her what the toilet paper is for. Show her how you wash your hands afterwards. Make going to the toilet a natural and normal part of life – nothing to be ashamed of or disgusted by.

Q *We have been trying to potty-train our three-year-old son off and on for six months now. Nothing seems to work, and he's still in diapers. He will go for a pee on the toilet if you catch him in time, but otherwise he's happy to wet or soil his diaper. Please help. We're expecting another baby in a few months.*

A I get many letters like yours. Potty-training causes parents a lot of anxiety and when parents are anxious, kids pick up on that fast. Parents need to relax and show their kids that bodily functions are natural and nothing to be embarrassed about. It's part of life. If you see the arrival of another baby as a deadline, that will just pile the pressure on and your son will be more resistant.

It may well be that you started the training before your son was really ready. No two kids are the same. Some kids are ready at two and a half or even earlier; others take longer to reach that point. But I think the key to your lack of success so far is there in the words "off and on." Stopping and starting training is not going to help your child get the message, and gives him control of the situation.

Here's what I would do:

★ Explain to your son that we're going to use the potty now because he is a big boy.

★ Get him out of diapers during the day and put him into underpants. Full stop! I'm not a believer in pull-ups – halfway houses only confuse the issue. Go to town when you buy him some underpants – underpants with designs that feature favorite TV or movie characters are really special for small children. Until he is succeeding during the day, keep him in diapers at night. You need to see him go through several nights without wetting his diaper before he's ready for the next stage.

★ During the training period, dress him in practical clothes, such as pants with elastic waists that can be pulled down quickly. Or if the weather is warm, let him run around in his underwear or shorts. Don't make it harder than it needs to be.

★ Equip yourself, if you haven't done so already, with two potties – one for in the house and a travel potty. These should be plain and simple, nothing fancy. At the same time, get a child's toilet seat. Some kids are frightened of falling into the toilet; some are scared of the flush. Offer your son the option – he can go in the potty or he can go on the toilet.

★ Keep track of his fluid intake, especially before bed. Learn his body patterns. Don't offer lots of drinks last thing at night, and avoid apple juice. It's a diuretic.

★ Watch over him throughout the day so you can learn to spot the signs when he needs to go. Ask him at regular intervals if he needs to go, but especially first thing in the morning on waking, after meals, before bedtime, and before leaving the house.

★ Repetition is the key. "Do you need to go pee pee?" Over and over again.

★ Explain to him what it feels like to want to go. You don't have to go into a huge amount of detail, just explain that he will feel an urge in his tummy lower down.

★ When he does go on the potty or the toilet, give him space. Don't hover over him or be intrusive. Some kids are shy in this situation. Let him take his time.

★ Every time he goes, give him lots of praise and encouragement. Keep a star chart so he can see that he's making progress.

★ Expose your son to different situations outside the home. Don't set him up for failure by going on long trips or outings, but take him for a short trip in the car or to the park and take the travel potty with you. He needs to learn how to pay attention to those urges and communicate them with you.

★ Never scold or blame your son when he has an accident. It's not a big deal. Accidents often happen when kids get distracted. Take the initiative and suggest that he goes to the toilet before he gets engaged in a new activity or before you leave the house together. Those parents who put a diaper on a potty-trained child when they go on a car journey really drive me nuts!

Q *My four-year-old son is dry during the day and at night. But he still sometimes soils himself, and it makes him really upset.*

A Some kids get the hang of bowel control before bladder control; for some it's the other way around. Bowel movements can make children anxious – it may be the feeling of passing a motion that makes them scared, or the result. Either way, they hold on until they have an accident.

Try to see if you can find a pattern here. Like bedwetting, soiling occurs at periods of disruption, stress in the family, or big changes, such as the arrival of a new sibling or moving house. Is there anything that could be upsetting him?

Soiling can also accompany illness or dietary changes. Have you introduced new foods into his diet recently? Could he be allergic to a particular food? Or is he constipated? If so, you will see the strain on his face when he tries to go. Check that he's eating plenty of fruit and vegetables and drinking enough fluids, or try putting him in a warm bath to relax his muscles and hurry things along. Eliminate all possible causes for the behavior.

The best way of dealing with this type of problem is to keep your response low-key. Prepare for possible accidents by keeping clean underpants, pants, and wet wipes on hand so you don't have to turn the house upside down to deal with them. Allow him enough time on the potty. Show him by your behavior that it's nothing to be anxious about.

Don't discipline him when he has an accident or go too far the other way and soothe him excessively. Simply note what's happened, then clean him up and don't pay him extra attention. Say to him: "You had the accident because you tried to hold it. Never mind. Next time, see if you can make it to the potty or the toilet." When he does manage to go on the potty or toilet, give him plenty of praise.

Q My three-year-old won't let me dress her without a fight. But she's reluctant to do anything for herself. Even putting on her shoes is a struggle. She kicks and lashes out, and then runs off screaming. What should I do?

A At three, your daughter is old enough to start to dress herself. Some of the willfulness that she's displaying in this area is down to her natural drive for more independence. You should be encouraging this, and not hold her back from the skills she needs to learn.

Many parents are reluctant to let kids dress themselves because it inevitably takes more time and effort on their part. Build the time into your schedule so that you can involve her in the process. Show her how to do up her buttons or pull on her top. Use plenty of praise. "Can you put your arm in the sleeve? Good girl!" "Let me see you put your socks on. Hold your sock like this and wiggle your toes down to the bottom!" Make it lighthearted and a game. Show her how the strap on her shoe goes through the buckle. Ask her to try. Break it down into small steps, and praise her along the way. I call this the **Big-Boy/Big-Girl Technique,** and it's ideal for making toddlers more independent and giving them a sense of achievement.

At the same time, it is important to demonstrate that you will not tolerate aggressive behavior from her. If she kicks you or runs away having a screaming tantrum, use the Naughty-Step Technique (page 172) or whichever version of it works best for you.

P is for Praise.
Give your kids plenty of praise when they do well. Reward good behavior with positive affirmation.

Q *What do you do with a faddy dresser? Whatever the occasion, it's got to be jeans or pants for my nine-year-old daughter and one of her three favorite tops – you can imagine the washing! She has lots of nice things, but I just can't seem to get her to wear them. I'd love to see her in a nice dress once in a while.*

A Who has a problem here, you or your daughter? She's choosing clothes that she likes and that make her feel comfortable. Let her. Provided she's dressing appropriately for the weather, don't expect her to share your taste or dress the way you would like her to dress. Lighten up a bit and don't take it so seriously.

A true faddy dresser isn't a child who is expressing her own tastes; it's a child who'll only wear blue, or green, or red, or who wants to wear the same top day after day after day. These obsessions need to be nipped in the bud before they take root by removing the clothing in question and offering the child no choice at all for a while.

In the case of your daughter, I wouldn't worry about trying to get her into a dress if she doesn't want to wear one. But I would get her to widen her choice. Ask her to find another four tops to add to the three so you can get through the week without having to run another wash.

Q *Our kids, Nina aged four and Nathan aged six, are nightmares to get dressed. They reject everything we suggest, and wind up choosing the most unsuitable clothes. The other day my son went to school wearing nothing but a T-shirt under his coat in sub-zero weather!*

A There's a simple way around this problem, and it's to sort and separate your kids' clothes into seasons. If it's winter, put the summer clothes into storage; if it's summer, put the winter clothes away. You could also separate casual clothes from more dressy items. Make sure your kids have separate drawers or wardrobes.

Tip: Do you want to wear the blue pants today?
Don't offer a toddler too much choice over what he wears. Small children haven't yet got the powers of reasoning to make sensible decisions about what they should wear. The night before, lay out his clothes for him – two choices at most.

Q *My little girl, who's two, absolutely hates having a bath. What do I do?*

A Is it the bath that bothers her? Or having her face and hair washed? Do you bathe her with your other kids? Is the bath too crowded to be comfortable? Is the water too hot or too cold? Is she scared of water? Or does bathtime represent bedtime to her? The first thing you have to do is identify the reason why your daughter doesn't want to have a bath.

Here are some ways to make bathing more pleasant for her:

★ Make sure you tell her when bathtime is coming up. Give her warnings before the event so she has time to prepare herself mentally. Some kids may give the impression that they hate baths, when what they're really doing is registering a protest at being caught unaware by a change in activity. You have to prepare them in the same way when it's time to get out of the bath.

★ Use a non-slip mat in the bath to prevent accidents. And make sure the water is not too hot.

★ If hair washing is a problem, get your child a hair shield to stop water and shampoo running down her face and getting into her eyes. Some kids are scared of shower nozzles. Use a cup instead, and say when you're going to pour the water.

★ Make bathtime fun with colorful games and toys – get her really enjoying herself! Bubble bath is also exciting for small children – and even for grownups! Just watch out for sensitive skins.

★ If your child shows she has a real fear of water – and fear is an emotion that is difficult to hide – don't force the issue. Build up her confidence by standing her up in a few inches of water and sponging her to wash her. Take every opportunity to have fun with water – splash through the rain in wellies, take her swimming, take her into the bath or shower with you. Then once she is more confident, gradually fill up the bath.

★ Let them be in control – especially if they're insecure in the water.

P is for Promise.
A promise is only a promise when it's kept.

ASK SUPERNANNY HOME AND AWAY

Q *However hard I try, I can't get our three kids (aged five, seven, and ten) up, dressed, and ready for school on time. Mornings are just chaos. What are we doing wrong?*

A Do you allow enough time? Adults can get up, get washed and dressed, and stumble out of the house in no time flat if they have to. Kids often take longer to get ready. Build the time into your schedule so you aren't rushing every morning or hurrying the kids along, which will only make them dig their heels in. Make sure your kids aren't getting to bed too late. Sleep deprivation means slow starts in the morning.

You can also help matters by preparing the night before. Try the **Rise-and-Shine Technique** to encourage your kids to take responsibility and become more independent.

HOW THE TECHNIQUE WORKS

★ Give each of your children their own alarm clock and lamp.

★ Write down the morning routine and stick it up next to the alarm clocks so that the children know what's expected of them and what steps to follow.

★ Let each child pick out an outfit or uniform the night before. Get their schoolbags ready.

★ In the morning, Mom or Dad goes into each child's room before the alarm goes off and does a "pre-wake." Turn on the lamp and gently nudge the child awake. Remind him that he has to get up when the alarm goes off.

★ When the alarm goes off, each child must get out of bed, get washed and dressed, come down for breakfast, then brush his teeth and get ready for school.

★ The key aspect of the technique is to give your kids plenty of praise and encouragement when they successfully complete a step in the routine.

I tried this technique with the Minyon family. When I arrived, I was surprised, to say the least, to see that seven-year-old Frank still wasn't dressing himself. It was sheer laziness on his part, coupled with the fact that he hadn't been given enough encouragement. Skyler, the four-year-old, kicked up such a fuss every morning that getting her out of the house could take well over an hour. Mom had to learn to stand her ground and leave the kids to get on with dressing themselves – not easy when you're used to constant battles. Skyler carried on testing her mother's control of the situation, but Danielle followed through – and one morning Skyler found herself being taken to school in her pajamas! That finally got the message across.

Another version of the Rise and Shine Technique is the **Get-Up-and-Go Chart**. The basic idea is the same – you prepare your kids' clothes and schoolbags the night before and encourage them to follow each step in the routine, only in this case you use a picture chart. Along the top of the chart are pictures that show each step the child has to follow: get up, get washed, get dressed, eat breakfast, brush teeth. Each time a child completes a step, she moves a picture of herself under the picture that corresponds to that particular step. Both parents need to give constant praise and encouragement when the steps of the routine are successfully completed. The key word is "responsibility." You're encouraging your kids to acquire important life skills.

Tip: Get organized!

If you have problems getting yourself and your kids out of the house on time, don't make things harder than they need to be. Get yourself ready first and keep your keys, handbag, shoes and so on, in one place so you don't have to rush around the house looking for them. If you've got a bathroom downstairs, keep a spare set of toothbrushes and face wipes there so the kids can quickly clean themselves up after breakfast.

Q *Now that they're a bit older, I let my boys go and play outside by themselves as we're near a playground. Recently they've been staying out later and later and refusing to come in when I call them. Should I withdraw the privilege and insist they stay indoors unless I go out with them?*

A Kids need fresh air, and they need plenty of time to run around outside to let off steam. In your case, I wouldn't withdraw the privilege. Instead, I would teach them that they must come in when you say so.

The technique I would use is the **Trust Technique**. It's a version of the Roaming Technique (page 136), but for older kids who can tell the time.

HOW THE TECHNIQUE WORKS

★ Make sure each child has a watch, and the watches are set to the same time.

★ Tell your kids that they can go out and play for 15 minutes and that when 15 minutes are up, they must come inside.

★ When they return after 15 minutes, tell them they can go out for another 20 minutes. A small increase in time builds up trust.

★ The reward for doing as you say is more play. Keep on with the technique until you build up the trust again.

Q *My little boy Mikey has this really bad habit. He's always running off when we're out in the park. He'll do it in the mall, too. I'm so scared I'm going to lose him one day or he'll hurt himself. He just thinks it's funny and won't listen to me. He's four, and he won't sit in the stroller any more.*

A Toddlers and small children often test their parents' limits in this way. Of course your son thinks it's funny when you catch him after he's run off. It's a game of chase to him – and it's getting him plenty of attention.

You need to teach your son that he should not run off where you can't see him. He needs to understand that this could be dangerous. At the same time, he is old enough to be given a little more freedom. I'm not surprised he won't sit in the stroller any more. He's not a baby. The mere fact that he's four years old tells me you're using the stroller as a way to restrain him. No wonder he takes off like a greyhound out of the trap!

One of the solutions I use on *Supernanny* is the **Roaming Technique**.

HOW THE TECHNIQUE WORKS

★ Tell your son that he can walk by himself, but he has to stop and stay where he is when you put up your hand and say "STOP." Use a low, authoritative voice. Don't let him hear anxiety in your tone, or anger, or fear.

★ Let him go a little way ahead and then say "STOP." If he stops and waits for you, praise him and let him carry on as before. If he doesn't stop, fetch him and make him hold your hand or sit in the stroller for four minutes.

★ Then when the four minutes are up, allow him to walk by himself again.

★ This technique gradually builds up trust. He will see that he can have his freedom within limits, and you will have given him more independence to boost his self-esteem.

Tip: Stop!
If your kids stray into areas in the home where you don't want them to go unsupervised – like your study, the garage, or home workshop – don't lock the doors. Instead, put a big STOP sign on each door and teach them that when they see that sign, they have to come and find an adult before they can go into the room. This teaches them responsibility. You can also put up a STOP sign on the inside of the front door if you've got escape artists on your hands, but in this case, you must lock the door as well. You don't want them running the risk of getting hit by a car or having an accident.

Q *Our kids are pretty well-behaved at home. Outside, it's a different story. We can't take them anywhere without them acting up – but they're really awful when we're out shopping. Once we leave the house, they just seem to turn into these wild crazy beings from another planet. It's driving my wife and me nuts.*

A I can't tell you how many letters and emails I get from parents in the same situation. Kids OK at home, different story in public. Why is this such a common problem?

I think one of the things parents have to do in this situation is to look at their own behavior when they're out with their kids. What do you do when your children start to act up? Discipline them? Or shrink with embarrassment and wish the ground would swallow you up? Parents often signal that they expect the worst as soon as they leave the house: "We're going to the supermarket and I don't want you to act up this time!" That's just setting them up to misbehave.

If your kids are behaving well at home, you've obviously got some discipline in place. Why don't you follow through using the same methods when you're out in public? In this type of situation, I teach parents how to use a Traveling Naughty Mat to curb bad behavior outside the home – the rules are exactly the same as they are for the Naughty Step (page 172). It doesn't matter where you are. Usually the biggest hurdle parents have to overcome is their own embarrassment.

But think about it for a moment. What's more embarrassing – taking a backseat while your kids have a meltdown, or stepping up to the plate and taking responsibility for controlling their behavior? Don't worry about the way other people react. These are your kids, not theirs.

At the same time, parents often make things more difficult than they have to be by expecting too much from their kids.

Here are some other things to think about:

★ Choose the right time for your outings – not when mealtimes or naptimes are going to be disrupted. For example, taking your kids shopping when they're already tired or have been at school all day isn't fair. Kids are more likely to have tantrums and misbehave when they're tired and hungry.

★ Don't break promises. If you've told your kids you'll take them to the park after you've done the supermarket shopping, follow through and give them their treat. Don't cut corners because it suits you.

Tip: Eating out
Don't expect small kids to be able to sit through a restaurant meal without some means of distraction. Take coloring books, pads of paper, and markers. Be realistic about the type of restaurant you take them to and the amount of time you spend there. No kid is going to sit there good as gold while you chat with your best friend for hours.

★ If you take your kids to a show, explain beforehand what it's going to be like. I've seen parents haul their kids along to concerts and shows that are obviously going to stretch them to the limit in terms of their behavior. Try to see it from your kids' point of view. They may well look forward to a show and then find when they get there that it's all a bit overwhelming – hundreds of people, lots of noise, and they've got to sit still for a long, long time. Prepare them before you get there. If their attention span is short, don't expect them to sit through a long show or a movie. Take them to something more suited to their age – it's why puppet shows only last half an hour or so.

★ When you're in the supermarket, try the **Involvement Technique** to stop them from running riot. If your kids can read, write down a list of items they have to find on the shelves and put in the cart. Give each child their own list. For small kids who can't read yet, you can draw pictures of the items you want them to get – bananas, bread, milk, orange juice. Make sure you include items from different aisles so they keep going with the technique all the way around the supermarket.

Sometimes, I give kids different tasks to do. In the Bixley family, for example, I gave Zack, the younger boy, the task of finding items and putting them in the cart, while the older boy, Brandon, added up the prices on a pocket calculator. These two kids had been supermarket terrors up until then, but the technique worked like a charm. They were really pleased with themselves.

Malls are also places where kids find it hard to control themselves. The young ones are tempted to run off in every direction, and the older ones are bombarded with the sight of lots of stuff they'd love to have. It's sensory overload. Be clear about what you're shopping for before you leave the house: "We're going to get a present for Grandma's birthday and a new bathrobe for Dad. I'm not buying any toys today, but I'll take you swimming after we've shopped." Set clear limits. Window shopping is not really a concept small kids understand. But, hey, a small treat never hurt anyone.

Tip: On vacation

Think about what your kids can realistically cope with when you're on vacation or having a family outing. Try to keep mealtimes and bedtimes in place. If it's 8:00 p.m. and your child has fallen asleep in his stroller while you finish your supper, that's fine. But keeping kids up until 11:30 at night is not fair on them. Use the hotel baby-sitter.

Q My kids (aged seven and five) always fight in the car, especially when we go to visit my parents, who live about an hour-and-a-half's drive away. By the time I get there, I'm absolutely fed up with their behavior and feel like turning around and going home again.

A Nine times out of ten, kids misbehave in cars because they're bored. They know you've got your eyes on the road and this gives them the perfect opportunity for a little sibling-bashing – anything to liven things up a bit. Think about it from their point of view. An hour and a half is a long time to sit strapped in a car seat without anything else to do. One recent survey, supported by the charity Raising Kids, reported that kids can only stand 12 minutes in the car before boredom sets in. Twelve minutes? That's not going to get you past the first traffic light.

The best way of dealing with this kind of behavior is to prevent it in the first place.

Here are some ideas you can try:

★ Story tapes are great for keeping kids absorbed in a world of their own. Or make a tape of their favorite songs and get them to sing along. It doesn't just have to be nursery rhymes or kids' songs. Old pop songs are fun to sing and make the miles go faster.

★ Try a bingo game. Give each child a bingo card with pictures of the types of things they can see out of the car window. Every time they spot an item shown on the card, they put a check next to it.

★ Get your kids to spot number plates. How many plates from different countries or states can they spot? How many letters? Can they get the whole alphabet?

★ You can't turn around and engage with your kids when you're driving. But you can still talk to them. I visited a family called the Amarals once. The three boys really acted up in the backseat during car trips, constantly whacking each other over the head. All it took to change the behavior was for Dad to initiate a conversation about the landscape they were driving through. Before long the kids were asking questions and really engaging with the answers. Pick a topic and see where it takes you.

Tip: Travel hints
If you're taking kids on a long journey by car, make sure you break the trip every couple of hours or so to give the kids the chance to stretch their legs, run off a bit of steam – and, of course, to go to the bathroom!

Keep your kids amused on train and plane journeys with a travel bag with games and activities – puzzles, crayons and paper, stories, and travel sets of favorite games. Or buy them a special treat (a new toy, for example) and give it to them halfway through as a surprise.

Q *My five-year-old daughter finds it difficult to settle in new places. Then, when it's time to go, she doesn't want to leave. The last time we went to my friend's house, I had to carry her kicking and screaming to the front door.*

A First of all, it's important that you don't cut down on social occasions or outings because of your daughter's behavior. She needs to learn how to behave outside the home and how to feel comfortable in new places. You have to keep exposing her to different situations to build up her confidence.

Help her to settle in a new place quicker by sitting down with her and engaging in some play alongside other children until she's playing happily. The quicker she settles, the less likely she'll feel robbed of playtime when it's time to go home. Try the same outing or activity or visit the same family for a while to get her used to the experience.

Take a look at your own behavior. How do you act when you go somewhere for the first time? Are you confident and calm, or are you apprehensive? Kids pick up many clues from their parents' behavior. Set a good example and she may learn to be less clingy and fearful. Don't pay her extra attention when she's clingy, or you will be rewarding her for the behavior you want to change.

When it's time to leave, give your daughter several reminders. Kids don't easily stop what they're doing and move on to the next activity. Tell her that it will be time to go in five minutes. Then tell her it will be time to go in three minutes, and she needs to put on her coat, or shoes, and come and say good-bye. Keep a running commentary going before you leave so she has a chance to prepare herself.

Q is for Quality Time.
Parenting may be hard work, but it isn't a chore. Cherish your special moments.

Q My four-year-old starts nursery next month. How do I prepare him for his first day?

A More to the point, how do you prepare yourself? That's normally the real question I'm answering.

The first day at school can be overwhelming for parents and their kids. Suddenly there's a new routine, new faces, and new experiences for your child to deal with. And for you it marks the end of one stage and the beginning of the next. Most parents can't help but feel a lump in the throat when their "baby" goes off to school for the first time. Remind yourself that while you may be feeling mixed emotions, you need to present a calm and confident manner to your child so he doesn't pick up on any stress or anxiety. Some kids take to school like ducks to water; others take more time to settle in. If you show your son that you find the whole experience earth-shattering, it will rub off on him.

Here's how you can ease the transition:

★ Visit the nursery and show your son around – where the coats go, where the story corner is, where the bathrooms are, what kind of activities go on. Talk to your child about all the exciting things he's going to be doing. Many nurseries have open days when kids can get acquainted with the facilities – if that's not the case, you can always ask if you could bring him in one day.

★ If you haven't done so already, get your child used to being left with caregivers for short periods during the day. Book a baby-sitter or ask a family member to come to your house and look after him for a while – or better still, arrange to take him to a friend's house or a family member's house so he gets used to the idea of being without you in less familiar surroundings.

★ Make sure you have established a good bedtime routine so that he is getting the sleep he needs. Trying to settle an overtired child at nursery school is an uphill struggle.

★ Practice your morning routine, too. Use the Rise-and-Shine Technique (page 134) if your son has trouble getting himself dressed and ready in the morning.

★ Try some role-play. Let your son be the Teacher. There are also some good children's books that you can read together to prepare him for the new experience.

★ Once he starts nursery school, make the effort to have parents and kids over after school.

Q *What do you do when your delightful seven-year-old girl suddenly starts behaving like an adolescent and discovers sarcasm in a big way? The Naughty Step has ceased to be effective. What measures can you take without being too heavy-handed?*

A Sarcasm is one of those gray parenting issues that is defined within each family. In some families, it's part of their humor.

But sarcasm isn't always funny. It's a matter of tone and intent. Sometimes it's backtalk, designed to be wounding and disrespectful. When your daughter is sarcastic with you, decide which it is – an attempt to be funny or plain rudeness.

"Yeah, right." "Whatever." Kids pick up this kind of lazy language from TV, books, and films – it's all around them in our culture. But it's also something they learn from their peers – and their parents. Do you use sarcasm yourself? Has she picked it up at home? Listen to your own tone of voice and make sure you are not setting her a bad example.

If your daughter is using sarcasm to be rude, you have to show her that it's not OK to speak to you like that, or she might start speaking like that to other people – teachers, friends, or relatives. The next time your daughter talks to you that way, tell her she is not to use that tone of voice to speak to you. You could try playing her behavior back to her in an animated way and show her what you mean. Copy the way she talks. Tell her that being sarcastic is disrespectful to you.

I don't see any reason why you should not remove a privilege and ask her to think about her inappropriate tone of voice. It's not about being heavy, it's about teaching your child how to behave around other people, including yourself.

R is for Respect.
Provide your kids with the guidance they need to respect themselves and others.

Q *Our four-year-old son has started to tell lies. He never admits if he's done something wrong, even when we catch him red-handed. What do we do? Do we discipline him for lying?*

A When we teach a child not to lie, what we are really teaching him is to be accountable for his actions. Very small kids find it hard to separate fact from fantasy. Your son is old enough and smart enough to have worked out that lying gets him out of a sticky situation.

The way you communicate with him is key. When parents demonstrate that they are very angry – "Did *you* do that?" – kids are tempted to lie out of fear. Instead, encourage him to open up. "Mommy wants to know the truth about what really happened here." Carry on disciplining him when he misbehaves and make sure that he apologizes for what he's done. But don't discipline him a second time for lying, label him, or confront him angrily. Instead, tell him that it's good to tell the truth and be honest with people. It's a moral issue.

Some kids lie in order to get attention when they feel they are short-changed. When I visited the Tsironis family, four-year-old Kate regularly reported foot cramps. The pain seemed real enough, just like the tears rolling down her face. But with her parents' attention taken up with very demanding three-year-old twin boys, Kate's foot cramps seemed to me like an immediate way for her to put herself back in the picture. I took her to one side and asked her whether her foot was really hurting or was it a way of getting Mom to give her cuddles. Kate didn't go so far as to admit that the foot cramps weren't real. She didn't have to – it was evident! But she did say: "I just want to be with my Mommy."

S is for Sharing.
Sharing is the key to social skills and building strength in relationships.

Q It's a real struggle to get my eight-year-old son to do his homework. No matter how much I nag him to get started with it, he leaves it to the last minute at night, by which time he's too tired to concentrate properly. His teacher says he's not doing as well as he should be.

A It may be your son's homework, but as a parent, you still have to take the lead here. Nagging isn't going to do it. Letting the bedtime routine fly out the window isn't going to help, either.

Set aside a time within your routine for your son to tackle his homework. Give him an hour or so to let off steam after school and enjoy himself, then sit him down in a quiet spot and get him started on his homework before supper and leave him to get on with it.

Is he finding his homework too hard? Is he taking too long to finish it? Work with his teacher and if he's having problems in a particular area, look for ways in which you can support him at home.

Q Our pre-teens are well-behaved most of the time and fun to have around. But I just can't get them to help out around the home. Are they being lazy, or should I just let them enjoy their childhood while they can?

A It all depends on whether it's causing a problem or not. If you're happy and they're happy, it's OK. In large families, many kids have no option but to help out more.

What your kids aren't learning, however, is how to take responsibility for themselves. They need the chance to begin to acquire those skills they'll need one day when they've left home. Don't wait until they've gone to college before you teach them what the buttons on the washing machine are for!

There are plenty of simple jobs they can do: pick up after themselves, make their beds, take out the garbage, set the table, help in the garden . . . Tackling chores successfully can be a great way of boosting kids' confidence and self-esteem. Make a chart listing the kind of chores you expect your kids to do. They can tick them off when they've completed them. Then you can add a positive comment to encourage them to continue. Once everyone's involved, family life becomes much easier. It's just another way of being together.

5 Stuff Happens

Life isn't easy sailing. Every family is going to find itself with a spanner in the works some time. Often what happens is out of your control. That's reality. When the unexpected happens, how do you cope with it? How do you guide your kids through difficult times? How do you encourage them to think for themselves and make good judgments and decisions?

At times of crisis, your children will look to you more than ever. It can be trying, when you are pushed to the limit yourself, to give them the support and the nurturing they need. You're going to have to take every opportunity to get some support for yourself, if necessary, so you can work through testing times to the best of your ability. This may come in the form of special groups, helplines or message boards, charities or agencies, doctors, church ministers, friends or family members, or a combination of any of the above. What's important is that you recognize that there is no need to struggle on alone. Putting the right support in place, so that your family doesn't suffer more than it absolutely has to, is all part of what it takes to be a committed parent. It's not a sign of weakness or failure to put your hand up and ask for help. After all, it's why this book was conceived.

Even when you are in a dark tunnel, having someone who will listen to you is very important. While those emotions you are feeling are isolating – and others might not truly know what you're going through if they haven't had the same experience – a sympathetic ear can be enough to keep you going. When you are dealing with a crisis,

it's not just time management that you need to put in place, it's energy management. The right support can help to put something back in the bank so that you can carry on.

The situation may be negative, but that doesn't mean it has to have a negative impact. A crisis shakes a family up, but it can be a positive experience, too. Good things can come out of it. Pulling together to get through the hard times often makes families stronger in the long run. You will stand a better chance of this if you take responsibility where necessary and don't give in to blame or let guilt cloud the issue. Stuff happens. I've seen parents beat themselves up years after an event took place that was completely out of their control – a hard birth, a life-threatening childhood illness, a diagnosis of special needs. But even when parents can identify issues they should have dealt with better, blame and guilt don't solve the problem in hand. We make mistakes. We're human. How we deal with the situation at hand is more important than dwelling on the past, refusing to let go or trying to rewrite history.

I strongly believe that a mistake is not a mistake if you learn from it. Imagine you are going down a road, you come to a junction and take the left turn. It leads to a dead end. So you turn back and go the other way. Life's the same. It's only a mistake if you keep taking that turn that leads to a dead end over and over again.

When you're stressed out dealing with a problem that's come out of the blue, it can make you put your kids on the back burner while you deal with what's blazing away in the foreground. You may tell yourself that what's happening doesn't affect them or will sail over their heads because they're too little to understand. This is not the case. Kids seem to have sixth senses sometimes – they pick up everything that's going on – if not from what you say, then from your tone of voice or your body language. Don't underestimate them. Don't air differences, disagreements, distress, or anxiety in front of them – keep your adult conversations for neutral ground out of their earshot. Try to stick to your routine as much as possible to keep your family framework in place. And, within reason, explain to them what's going on in simple terms that they can understand, without recourse to anger, blame, or trying to make the other parent look bad. Silence just encourages kids to fill in the gaps. You may think that you are sparing your kids, but their imaginations will be in overdrive. "Mom and Dad are sad and unhappy. Is it my fault?"

In times of trouble, children often blame themselves. They may start to be more challenging in their behavior – or they may go to the opposite extreme and become unnaturally "good" because of the instability that they sense in the home. You need to reassure them with comforting words that they have done nothing wrong, and still be a parent to them. At the same time, don't load your kids up with information or unnecessary facts that are not relevant to them. Or worse, fall into the trap of seeking comfort from them. You're the adult. Don't make your kids take on a grown-up role. If you put your kids in the position of having

to support you like a friend, or load them up with too much detail, you're storing up trouble for later on.

Problems and the stress that comes with them can leave you at sea, uncertain which direction to take. When it's blowing a gale, you may find yourself disagreeing with your partner about how best to handle things. Before you know it, no one's sailing the ship. Now more than ever, it is important to take the time to sit down and discuss the issues at hand and come up with a common approach. It's about the kids, after all.

Topics and techniques covered in this chapter:

MOVING – preparing the children

FAMILIES UNDER PRESSURE – juggling with too many balls

THE INVOLVEMENT TECHNIQUE – preparing your child for a new baby in the family

SEPARATION AND DIVORCE

BECOMING A STEP-PARENT

CHILDREN WITH SPECIAL NEEDS

BEREAVEMENT – how to help your children cope

Q *My husband's new job means that we will have to relocate to another part of the country. I'm worried about the effect this will have on our three kids. Aisha is eleven and has just started secondary school. Jared is eight, and Jay, the little one, is three. We haven't mentioned anything to them yet because the details have just been finalized, but now it looks as if we're going to have to move a little sooner than we thought. How do we break it to them that they will be starting new lives in a different place?*

A Something about the tone of your letter suggests to me that you're of two minds about the move yourself. I've seen a similar situation where a mother was so worried about how a forthcoming move would impact her two children that she went all out to pacify them. What this did was send a message that she hadn't fully embraced the decision herself.

Kids look to their parents in these kinds of situations, and if you're approaching the move with some reluctance, they're going to pick up on that, too. They may already sense that something's in the air – it's hard to keep big changes like a new job or moving completely under wraps. You may even find that your older two are more clued in than you think. Don't keep it under wraps any longer.

Before you tell them the news, sit down with your husband – preferably outside the house – and discuss ways in which you can stress the positive sides of the changes to come. What are the advantages of the new location? What new activities will your kids be able to enjoy? Equip yourself with as much local information as you can – which schools will your kids be attending? Where are you likely to be living? The more answers you can give your kids at this stage, the more confident they will be about the change. Moving house, moving school, and moving to a different area throw a lot of unknowns up into the air.

Call your kids together and put them in the picture. Be positive. Show them how much you are looking forward to the move. Tell them it will be an exciting new experience for the whole family. Be reassuring and confident. You are not selling them the idea: it's simply a fact and it's non-negotiable. Change unsettles many kids, some more than others. But coping with change is an important life skill. Even parents find it difficult sometimes. Show them that there are gains to be made, not just losses. Perhaps they will be able to have that dog they've been wanting at long last. Perhaps the new house will have a bigger garden. Perhaps you will be commuting shorter distances to work and will be able to spend more time with your family.

Help them put their worries into perspective. Point out that their old friends can come to stay, and that there are lots of ways they can still keep in touch. Tell them that they will make new friends, too.

Allow them time to digest the information and react to it in their own way – it's a big step, and they need to feel secure. Don't force the issue, but be on hand when they want to talk things over. Sometimes children will keep on worrying a subject like a dog with a bone if they don't get the answer they want. In that case, keep the conversation moving on and change the subject. After you have broken the news to them jointly, make sure you both spend time with each child on a one-on-one basis to keep the lines of communication open. Validate their feelings. At first, they may be afraid, angry, sad, or confused about what's going to happen, especially if you have never moved before. But don't necessarily expect the worst – you may find your kids are excited by the prospect of a change.

After the move, make sure you take every opportunity to get out and about and meet people. Follow up any invitations from neighbors, go to events at your kids' new schools, join clubs or take up activities that have a social side. Start putting down new roots. Some families react to a major move by isolating themselves in their family unit, which sends out the message to their kids that the new location is a threatening place. Stay positive and meet the challenges in a confident way, and your kids will be encouraged to follow your lead.

At the same time, allow them time to get used to their new home environment and get acquainted with their bedrooms and the layout of the new place. If possible, take the time to sort out your kids' rooms first before you unpack the rest of the boxes. Put out their toys and favorite things so they have their own little sanctuary and can start to settle down.

T is for Time.
Put the time into your parenting. Manage your time efficiently to keep chaos and disarray at bay.

Q *Two years ago, my husband left his job to start up a home business. Money's been pretty tight, so I've had to take on a part-time job to pay the bills until the business is on a more secure footing. Then, last April, our four-year-old daughter developed an eye problem, which has meant that she's been in and out of the hospital getting treatment. The condition is improving slowly, but I still have to take her for regular appointments at the clinic. Our problem is our son, Daniel, who's nine. He's been doing really well at school until just recently. Last week I was called in to see his teacher who said that he'd been fighting in the playground and talking back in class. I feel like a complete failure as a mother. I can't give up my job – but I can't be in ten places at once! What should I do?*

A Part-time job, hospital appointments, money worries, Dad working at home – you're carrying a lot of baggage here. And not just you, but the whole family. Moms are all too willing to take everything onto their own shoulders. You're not a failure, you're just overwhelmed.

When something like your daughter's eye condition happens out of the blue and a family is already stretched, it isn't easy to step back and see the big picture. But now that she is improving, you need to sit down with your husband and talk about ways in which you *two* can share the load. He may be working hard to establish his business, but at least he's home. His hours will be more flexible. Share the hospital visits between you and find other ways that you can work together to maintain the household

routine so that resentment doesn't build up.

Daniel is the missing piece of the puzzle here. Have you let things slip while you responded to your daughter's need for treatment? How much time do you spend with him on a one-on-one basis? Don't assume that his difficulties at school reflect what's happening at home. There could be other explanations – he might be struggling to keep up with his work or homework, he might be being bullied, he may not be getting enough attention in class . . . you need to root out what's going on at school to see the whole picture. A lot of busy parents operate on their own timetables when it comes to talking to their kids. "Right, that job's done. Now tell me what happened at school today." It may be a convenient time for you to talk, but your son won't necessarily open up on demand. Wait for the moment when he shows signs of being more forthcoming to have a full discussion.

When a family is under pressure, the first thing they cut back on is quality time. But quality time isn't an optional extra, it's a necessity. It's the glue that holds you all together and keeps you close. You and your husband need to spend quality time with each of your kids, together and on a one-to-one basis. You need to spend time as a couple. And you both need some "Me" time to recharge your batteries. Look at your daily routine and see what adjustments you can make so that you all have more breathing space.

It's all about priorities. Deal with what's important and comfort yourself with the thought that these periods of stress are generally short-lived. That perspective can be enough to get you through it.

Q *We're expecting a baby in four months' time. Is it too early to prepare my three-year-old daughter for the new arrival? And how should we do this?*

A Congratulations! A new baby is a blessing. You may think it's strange that I'm choosing to answer this question in a chapter that largely covers more difficult areas of parenting. But it is important to understand that the arrival of a new sibling can have a huge impact on a child's world, and it is totally up to us as adults to make it a positive change. You need to ease your daughter in gently and lay the foundations so that she will accept her new brother or sister in a relaxed and confident way. Prepare yourself well and you are less likely to have to cope with jealousy or regression on her part.

At the same time, be aware that, despite all your preparation, you won't know for certain how she will react until she is confronted with the reality of the new baby. Some kids greet the news that "Mommy's going to have a new baby" as if you had just told them you'd ordered a side salad. "Is the baby going back now?" That's not an unusual question to come out of the mouth of a new big sister or brother.

How do you go about preparing your child? You've made a good start by not raising the issue too early. Small children have very little sense of time – a week or two is ages to them. If she notices your bump and asks about it, that's a perfect opportunity to introduce the subject. Otherwise, the timing is up to you. You don't want to be answering questions for months while the wait stretches on and on for her, but on the other hand you need time to get her used to the idea and to be part of the pregnancy.

Explain to your daughter that she is going to be a Big Sister soon. Tell her that, when the new baby arrives, she's going to be a big help to you. Talk about what you'll be doing together after the baby is born. Little children often get anxious about a new arrival because they don't understand how the new dynamic is going to work or how the change will affect them. If she expresses worries, reassure her, but avoid putting ideas into her head or using her as a sounding board.

Let your daughter feel your stomach and feel the baby kicking. Show her your excitement and joy at the prospect of the new arrival. People are all too prepared to focus on the negative aspects and ignore the positive and happy message. There are lots of good children's books that cover the subject in a jolly and simple way, and these can be a big help in engaging her with the subject and putting her mind at rest. At the same time, don't give her more information about the actual process of birth than she can handle. She's bound to have lots of questions, but don't tell her anything that might make her concerned about you.

Now's also the time to encourage your toddler to be more self-sufficient and develop her life skills. Teach her how to dress herself and put on her shoes. Before the second child comes along, some parents are totally at the beck and call of their toddler. Then, when a new baby comes along, they step back and all of a sudden expect their toddler to do up the buttons on their own parka. Prepare your child by encouraging her to do small achievable tasks for herself.

When the big day (or night) eventually arrives, make sure you have put arrangements in place so that your child can be looked after by someone she knows and trusts while you are in the hospital. You might want to buy a few presents and a card to give her when she visits you for the first time.

Once, when I was looking after a little boy, we decorated a whole room in pink when his baby sister was born. It was a real birthday party, complete with cake. The little boy was so excited at taking part in the celebrations – and Mom burst into tears of joy as soon as she saw it.

After the baby is born, keep the focus on your daughter when she comes to see you in the hospital. It may well be her first night without you, or the first time she has spent the night away from home. It may be her first visit to a hospital. For all these reasons and more, she may be excited or feeling conflicting emotions. Pay her a lot of attention. Get her involved in the new shape of your family right from the start. One of the ways to do this is with the **Involvement Technique**.

Tip: I ♥ baby
Some parents can't imagine loving a second child as much as their first. Trust me, you will. As my Mom and Dad would say: "Your heart just gets bigger."

HOW THE TECHNIQUE WORKS

In the days and weeks that follow, make sure you stick to the routine you have established with your daughter as far as possible. It takes new babies a while to develop a settled pattern of feeding and sleeping, but don't abandon the structure you have already put in place or you will find yourself trying to manage chaos. Make sure your partner spends quality time with your daughter while you get the rest you need. When you have to tend to the baby, use the Involvement Technique to keep your daughter included. Ask her to fetch things for you and praise her when she does. Keep up a running commentary so she feels as if she is getting attention at the same time as the baby. When she helps you, tell her she is a "Big Girl" and that you are so proud of her. Dolls, toy baths, and other mini baby gear can also help. Praise her for the difference she is making.

A lot of parents notice that their older child regresses a little when a new baby arrives. To the older child, "baby" behavior might seem like the perfect way of getting more attention or putting herself on an equal footing – babies need to be held constantly, and small children read that as extra affection. The Involvement Technique can help to ensure that any regression is short-lived. If you praise your child for being a "Big Girl" and give her small tasks and responsibilities, she won't feel such a need to regress.

Q *After years of trying to make our marriage work, my husband and I have agreed to separate. How can we ensure that we cause the least amount of emotional damage to our kids? You read these terrible statistics about how much harm divorce does to children. Casey, our son, is seven, and Keri is ten.*

A You've reached the point of no return in your marriage, but you're still Mom and Dad to your kids. Those roles are for life. It's not so much the separation itself that damages kids, it's the way their parents go on to deal with subsequent issues like sharing the responsibility for their kids' care. The marriage is over, but your commitment to your kids remains.

What I hear from what you say is that you have reached a decision together as amicably as possible. That's important. The period of transition before a separation can be very damaging, especially if it is marked by a lot of hostility. When a marriage gets into difficulty, either you should resolve your differences, forgive, and move on, or take the decision to part. Drawn-out conflict is what does the most harm to children.

Now that you have reached your decision, what you must do as soon as possible is tell your kids what's happening. It's quite possible that they've picked up on the stress and tension already. Sit down together as a family and give them the facts. Explain in simple terms that you've both decided that it's best if you live apart. Tell them that you are still their parents and that you still love them just the same. Tell them that it's not

their fault if they ask. Many kids, especially small children, think that they've done something wrong when parents split up, especially if they have been used as a weapon in their parents' battles with one another, or if they have overheard conversations in which their names have been bandied about. They may blame themselves. They may try to be extra good because they think that will make their parents stay together. Even older children, who may be able to appreciate that the separation might be for the best in the long run, will still take the news like a blow to the heart. That's unavoidable, and you have to accept it.

Establish some ground rules about how you will behave in front of the children. Don't argue or fight in front of them. Don't break down in front of them. Be respectful and polite to one another. Repeated conflict or wounding behavior is very damaging for kids. Don't put your own emotions first or let kids hear too much.

If you have issues to resolve about finances, contact or living arrangements, discuss them out of earshot of the children. Mediators can be very helpful in getting couples to come to joint decisions about their futures in a setting that is not confrontational.

Listen to your kids and be understanding. Tell them that it's OK to be upset. Your children may find themselves feeling lots of different emotions – sadness, anger, fear, shame, guilt, and confusion. Help them air their feelings so they can get through this difficult stage. The situation needs to be addressed – you can't push it away. Keep others in the picture, too. Tell your children's teachers and any caregivers or family members they see on a regular basis. If you feel your kids are bottling things up at home, encourage them to talk to other people – it may help them to get their feelings off their chests. Grandparents, with their great reserves of love, patience, and understanding, can play a vital role here.

Keep other changes to a minimum. If at all possible, try to ensure that your kids can stay in the same school. In an ideal world, whether one parent is moving out of the family home, or both parents are setting up new households, you should try to stay as geographically close as possible so that you can share the care of your children more easily and their lives are not constantly disrupted by long trips up and down the highway.

After the separation:

★ Give your children plenty of time and attention.

★ Rebuild that trust.

★ Allow your children to have a close relationship with both of you. Don't make them take sides. Don't involve them in any issues you both still have, or any new ones that might arise (including new relationships). Don't badmouth each other.

★ Be consistent when it comes to raising your kids.

★ Keep each other informed – about the good things as well as the bad. Encourage your kids to keep in touch with the other partner while they're at your house.

★ Try to stick to your arrangements regarding contact as far as possible. Don't break arrangements without giving plenty of warning, or turn up late. If you break an arrangement without notice, your kids will think you don't want to see them. Be polite and respectful to each other in front of your kids.

★ Set aside time at regular intervals to review arrangements and incorporate any changes. Kids grow and develop, and you will need to be flexible to stay in step with their needs. Issues like school trips and finances may need to be discussed. There's no reason why two adults can't set aside their emotions and concentrate on what they have in common, which is their *children*.

Q I'm a few months into a new relationship with a single mom who I met at work (we're both in our late 20s). She has two sons, Jason (aged seven) and Christopher (aged five) – both nice boys. Their Dad left when they were very little and they've had no contact with him since. Julie and I have discussed living together – we'd both like to very much. The problem is Jason. He's wary of me and sometimes rude. What do you advise? The relationship is important to me. I love Julie and the boys so much, and want to be a good father figure to the lads.

A The first few months of a new relationship are a special time. Everything seems possible. But when there are kids already on the scene, you have to take things a little slower.

As these two kids have never been acquainted with their Dad, the role you will play in their lives will be very important. It will be great for the kids to have a male role model to look up to and identify with. But you've got to get the timing right. Even though you and Julie have not known each other for very long, you will still have had time to develop your relationship to some degree. Now you have to bring the boys into the picture so you are all on the same page.

Before you think about moving in, work on developing a relationship with the boys and Julie together. Mom has to take a bit of a lead here and give you the lowdown on her family so that you understand the dynamic. She should show her kids that they are not being neglected in favor of her new relationship. At the same time, she should

step back a little to allow the boys the chance to make the transition and get to know you.

Next, take the time to build up a relationship with each of the boys. Give them some one-to-one attention. Jump into their world. Take them on outings or share an activity with them. Or simply spend some time with them at home playing a game or kicking a football about. It's not about bribing them for their affection, it's just giving them the chance to accept you for who you are. Let them see that you are interested and engaged. Jason's wariness and his rudeness aren't directed at you personally – it's what you represent. He may be feeling jealous. Give him the chance to get to know you properly so that he sees you as an addition to his family, not as a loss of something important to him, which is his relationship with his mother.

When the kids are more used to having you around, you can take the next step. But give it time.

And when you do move in, accept the fact that you will have to have established a good relationship with both kids before Mom will accept you disciplining them. I worked with a family once where Mom did not allow the step-dad to discipline the oldest boy, who was a child of a previous relationship. That caused a lot of difficulties, not least with the child's behavior.

Talk to Julie about her parenting approach and build up a feel for those areas in which you agree and those where you don't. Sit down with Julie and agree a common approach. She's the expert on her kids, but you have an outside perspective.

Work together so the boys can't drive a wedge between you, and everyone should settle into the new family dynamic.

Remember, don't force the pace. Patience is the key.

Q Do your techniques work for children with special needs? I have a son of six who is showing clear signs of ADHD (Attention Deficit Hyperactivity Disorder). But he has the same kind of behavior issues – aggression and fighting – that I see on your program.

A We're all too quick to slap labels on kids these days. I would advise any parent in your position to work through all the possible reasons for the behavior first.

Children who regularly misbehave, who are particularly difficult, or who are not progressing as they should, are a worry to parents. All parents have heard that small nagging voice in the back of their head that tells them something isn't right. First, eliminate as many potential causes for your child's difficulties as possible. Diet is one – does your child react badly to certain foods? Deafness or a hearing difficulty can cause problems with language. An underlying medical condition can show up in unruly behavior. Some kids just take more time and effort to become engaged with the world.

If your child is diagnosed as having special needs, make sure he is fully assessed by a number of different professionals, not just a GP. For example, it can be useful to arrange for a therapist to observe your child at home. Or you may wish to consult an educational psychologist who can assess your child's behavior at school. Any diagnosis should be made in the round, taking in the whole picture.

If your son is diagnosed with ADHD, get as much information and support as you can. Read up on the condition, join a parents' group, or visit a message board to gain tips and advice from professionals and other caregivers.

I have worked with a number of families who had children with special needs. The Webb family's five-year-old daughter Paige has Downs syndrome. The Facente family's three-year-old son Tristram is autistic. I've also met kids with ADHD. In the case of the Webbs and the Facentes, I worked alongside the remarkable Dr. Lynn Koegel, a specialist in educational psychology at the University of California, who has run a training center for over 25 years that helps thousands of kids with different types of special needs.

What I have observed is that structure, routine, and consistency can be helpful, depending on the particular condition. Repetition, for example, is helpful for autistic children, and you can use picture charts to guide them through a daily routine. Structure is good for kids with ADHD because it helps to keep them focused. Many children with Downs syndrome don't like change, and consistency can be a real help here. A workable schedule will also allow you to spend more time giving your child one-on-one attention, while meeting the needs of your other kids, too.

I've also noticed that special needs children do better when you focus on their achievements, however small and slow the progress, and reward and praise them. Children who suffer from Asperger's syndrome often have very low self-esteem and respond well to praise. Kids with ADHD experience a lot of frustration, and small, achievable tasks will bolster their confidence. Encouragement is key.

Communication is often a source of frustration. Paige, for example, needed help to build up her vocabulary so she could be better understood. Her mother had gotten used to speaking for her, which meant that Paige was not making an effort to learn and use new words. Once Mom took the time to ask Paige different questions, introduce her to new words, and encourage her to practice her pronunciation, she became more fluent. In Tristram's case, it was a question of focusing on getting him to recognize his name, so we played a game to get him to come when he was called.

Kids with special needs can make really significant progress if you engage with them and move things along step by step. Private tutoring can also be a great source of help.

If you have a child with special needs, get him involved with family life and let him join in with shared play and games as far as possible. But sometimes it can also be important to give him his own space so that your other kids don't suffer. For example, bedtimes were a problem in the Webb household. Once I introduced the Stay-in-Bed Technique (page 96), the two other children, Josef and Madison, began to get the message. But Paige was not able to be that consistent. We moved the kids around to give Paige her own bedroom so that her siblings stood a better chance of following the bedtime routine.

When you're a parent of a child with special needs, bear in mind that there are some aspects of your child's behavior and development that you will not be able to change. But that does not mean that you should give up trying to encourage them to progress in whatever ways they can. Even what you consider to be a small improvement is still going in the right direction.

U is for Understanding.
Acknowledge your child's viewpoint and put yourself in their shoes.

Q *My wife's mother died unexpectedly last week. How do we help our kids cope with the loss of their beloved grandmother? We have three daughters, aged nine, five, and three.*

A I'm sorry to hear of your loss. This will be a sad and upsetting time for all the family, particularly your wife. How you deal with this will have a significant impact on yourself as well as the kids. Such devastating events, which are experienced every day by families, change the whole dynamic.

In adults, grief works through a number of stages. The first is shock – which will be heightened for you and your wife, as your mother-in-law's death was sudden. After shock comes an intense feeling of missing the person who's gone, then anger, guilt, and finally sadness and acceptance. Your grief will be different than your wife's. The death of a parent is a huge transition.

Like adults, kids feel a similar range of overwhelming emotions when they lose somebody close to them. But they may not know how to express their feelings. On the surface, they may appear not to be dealing with the situation at all, but recovery is a slow process, and much healing will be needed. How you support them at this time will make the transition easier.

Very young children don't really understand the concept of death. It's quite common for kids under five to think that the person will be coming back some time in the future, or to be curious about where that person has gone. Your three-year-old will know that Mom is upset and sad, and will be affected by what's going on in her immediate environment. She may understand that some big event has made Mom cry. She may repeat what she's overheard: "Nana's gone to heaven." But she is too young to have a real emotional grasp of what's happened. Your five-year-old is more likely to know that she won't see her grandmother again. Your nine-year-old most definitely will. I wouldn't necessarily advise allowing your two youngest children to go to the funeral, but it can be an important part of the grieving process for your nine-year-old.

Encourage your children to talk about how they feel. Spend time with each of them alone, and listen to what they say. Don't overload them with detail that is too upsetting, but make it clear that you are always there for them to talk to. Give them simple answers to their questions. Clarity and honesty is the key to helping your older children adjust to life without their grandmother.

Be on the alert for changes in behavior that might indicate a child is having difficulties expressing their feelings. Strong emotions sometimes cause young children to regress – they may wet the bed or become clingy. Older kids can become withdrawn, find it difficult to concentrate, or show signs of anxiety. Counseling can be very helpful in this situation. Having someone outside the home to talk to can be a good way for kids to release their feelings.

Bring out the photo albums and talk about the good times they've had with their grandmother. If you avoid all mention of

their grandmother, you will increase your
kids' fear and anxiety – it will become a taboo
subject. Listen, answer their questions, and
give them time to grieve in their own way.
When they do want to talk, it may be an
inconvenient time, but take advantage of it –
when the door's pushed open, it's open.

Don't try to conceal your own emotions at
this time and keep a stiff upper lip. Kids need
to see how you feel. A death in the family is a
fact that can't be dismissed or disguised. It
will take adjustment, and everyone will have
their own grieving time. Once you as parents
find equilibrium, your kids will also settle.
Every day helps build acceptance.

6 The Naughty Step and Beyond

Now that *Supernanny* has been on TV for a while, I'm beginning to come across families who have seen some of the early shows and who are putting the Naughty Step, or one of the variations of the discipline technique, into practice. It's fantastic that parents have been inspired by the program to try the techniques themselves. It's even more encouraging when they report that the techniques have worked, and that their family life has improved beyond recognition as a result.

But that isn't always the case. What's also been a bit of an eye-opener for me is the number of parents who try the techniques and don't get anywhere with them. Once or twice, I've even visited families on *Supernanny* who were already using the Naughty Step or something similar before I got there, but were making no headway with it. This has given me the opportunity to see firsthand where things have gone wrong. What I've learned is this: nearly every time the techniques haven't worked, it's because parents were ignoring the essential steps or had failed to follow through in some form or another.

One of the reasons for writing this book was to offer more detailed and in-depth instruction on the techniques I teach on the program. In this chapter, I'm going to enlarge on the methods I use when children misbehave, and then break the methods down stage by stage, so you can be sure of success when you use them.

To use any method successfully, you have to understand how and why it works. Once you've grasped the thinking behind it, you will be able to see why following the steps is crucial, and you will be less likely to undermine the technique by skipping a stage, changing the rules, or acting inconsistently.

We live in an age where everyone expects a quick fix. Lose weight fast! Instant results or your money back! See the difference in only seven days!

Well, raising kids is not like that. To correct a pattern of bad behavior, to teach your children to obey the rules and to respect you, to give them confidence and help them become more independent, takes time, commitment, and perseverance. You can't expect instant results, and you can't expect to find a solution without putting the work in. I see parents who for years have been dealing with situations that have robbed them of energy – then they use a technique and expect a quick turnaround. Put the time into your family, and don't expect changes to happen overnight.

Tip: *Know when not to discipline*

In some situations (while you might give your child a firm word), you shouldn't discipline her. Don't discipline your child if:

✴ *She's ill.*

✴ *In time of crisis in your family or major disruption – such as moving, illness or stress, or the arrival of a new baby. Cut her some slack when times are difficult or everything's up in the air.*

✴ *She is genuinely shocked at her behavior and sincerely sorry for what happened. If she is already upset, talk to her about what she did and why it happened, remind her of the rules, and leave it at that.*

✴ *You're not sure what happened. Most of the time, it will be crystal clear who is the guilty party, but if there is reasonable doubt, it's better to let the incident pass. Disciplining children repeatedly for things they haven't done encourages them to lie.*

✴ *She's already been disciplined once for whatever she did.*

Topics and techniques covered in this chapter:

THE NAUGHTY STEP AND VARIATIONS ON THE THEME to suit every situation

HOW TO DEAL WITH TANTRUMS in toddlers and older children

REFLECTION ROOM, COOL-DOWN AREA, AND CHILL-OUT ZONE for kids who have lost control

BREATHING TECHNIQUE for defusing anger in parents

THE ONE-STRIKE-AND-YOU'RE-OUT TECHNIQUE for children who are behaving badly to gain attention

THE TOY-CONFISCATION TECHNIQUE for kids who fight over toys

V is for Values.
Teach your kids your family values and what's important to you.

I believe that the **Naughty Step** – and all its variations – is one of the most effective ways of teaching a child that a particular behavior is unacceptable. Some people call it Time Out. Whatever you call it and whatever variation you use – chair, stool, spot, bench, point – the basic idea is the same. Techniques that I'll be explaining later for teaching children how to cool down after a tantrum or some other kind of outburst also share the same approach.

So what's the thinking behind it?

First, it's important to say what the Naughty Step *isn't*. It's firm control, but it isn't harsh punishment. You will not hurt a child by using this technique, and you won't crush his spirit, either. What the technique does is to allow a child to think about his actions and learn what happens if he misbehaves. It's all about getting children to think for themselves, take responsibility, and be accountable for their actions.

The basic idea behind the technique is to remove the child from the scene for a short while so he has a chance to calm down, think about what he's done, and apologize for his behavior. Why is it important to remove him from the scene? Because by removing him from the scene – even if he remains in sight – you are showing him that behaving badly is not the way to get attention. A lot of bad behavior is attention-seeking, so this aspect is very important. At the same time, removing him from the scene shows him that when he is naughty – when he bites, kicks, or lashes out – he can't carry on joining in family activities or doing what he was doing until he has sat out his time and apologized.

Bad behavior doesn't deserve company – it's socially unacceptable.

HOW THE TECHNIQUE WORKS. EACH STAGE IS IMPORTANT.

★ **THE WARNING** Your five-year-old daughter has kicked her three-year-old brother hard on the leg. The first step is to give her a Warning. Go to her, get down to her level and make eye contact. Use the Voice of Authority to tell her the behavior is wrong and why. Say: "That behavior is unacceptable. You don't kick your brother. Be kind to people. If you behave like that again, you're going to the Naughty Step." Only give one warning. Then walk away. Don't wait for a reaction.

★ **THE NAUGHTY STEP** A couple of minutes later, your daughter kicks her brother again. As soon as she does, take her straight to the step and sit her down.

★ **THE EXPLANATION** Explain to your daughter why she's been put on the step. Get down to her level. Say: "You don't kick your brother or anyone else. We don't hurt people. It's unacceptable behavior. Now you will sit here for five minutes* and think about what you've done."

★ **WALK AWAY** Don't engage further with your child, no matter what she's saying or doing. Walk away. If she gets up from the step, put her back.

*The number of minutes will depend on the child's age: two minutes for a two-year-old, three for a three-year-old, and so on. If your child is two and a half, go to the nearest level, based on a child's maturity.

★ **COME BACK AND EXPLAIN**

★ **THE APOLOGY** When five minutes is up, go to your daughter and get her to apologize. "I want you to say sorry." She must say what she is apologizing for.

★ **LET GO** Once she's apologized, say: "Thank you." Show her that you accept her apology. Use a higher tone of voice to show you're pleased. Give her a kiss and a hug. Invite her to join in with a family activity or to play as before.

Sounds simple, doesn't it? Let's look at the stages in more detail to see what can go wrong. On the following pages are some questions I'm often asked.

Q *Why should I bother giving my child a warning? Wouldn't it be better to take him to the Naughty Step straight away? I don't want to wait until he's hit his brother a second time before I discipline him.*

A There are several reasons why you should give your child a warning, but the most important is that it gives him a chance to understand that you're unhappy with his actions and to make a judgment and decide for himself to correct his behavior. If you skip the warning and march him straight to the Naughty Step, you've given him nowhere to go and no chance to redeem himself.

A warning is also vital because it identifies the bad behavior and tells him that he's crossed a line. Toddlers are like Curious George, creating mayhem out of their desire for exploration. Small children sometimes don't know that what they're doing is wrong. You have to tell them. Even when they do know they shouldn't do something, they may forget in the heat of the moment. You need to remind them of the rules. Say you're in the mall with your toddler and she suddenly spots Barney. She knows she shouldn't run off, but the impulse to greet her favorite character is just too great. Off she goes . . . You step in with the warning.

A warning tells the child that his behavior is unacceptable and why. It tells him that if he carries on, there will be a consequence. Sometimes, with some children, that's all it takes.

Q *How can I get my six-year-old son to listen to me? When I warn him that if he does something one more time he's going on the Naughty Step, he tunes me out or we end up having a shouting match.*

A Giving your son a warning is not the same as telling him off. Warnings tell children that they have crossed a line, and that they shouldn't behave that way in future. When your son tunes you out ("La, la, la, la, la" – fingers in the ears: I've seen that!) he's trying to control the situation. Of course that's going to aggravate you into justifying yourself. Why go there? Don't raise the bar. Say what you have to say and walk away.

What you say is very important. A warning should never be an excuse to lash out verbally. Say: "Snatching toys is unacceptable behavior. We don't snatch toys from people." Or: "We don't use bad words in this house. Swearing is unacceptable behavior." What you *shouldn't* say is: "NO! You bad, bad boy! I can't believe you did that! Stop it right now!" Your child is not a "bad boy." It's the behavior that is unacceptable. And how is he supposed to know what "that" and "it" is if you don't tell him?

Only give one warning. If you carry on warning your child, he's going to work out pretty quickly that you are just issuing empty threats. He'll ignore you, and you'll have undermined the technique before you've even started because he knows you won't follow through.

How you talk to your child is just as important as what you say. Small children watch our every move and copy our behavior.

Body language and tone of voice speak volumes to them, and may even communicate more effectively than the words you say.

When you are warning your child, or explaining to him why he's been put on the Naughty Step, go to him, get down to his level, and make eye contact. Parents often forget how big they appear to a small child looking up at them. Standing over a child while you warn them is unnecessarily intimidating. The point of a warning or explanation is not to frighten the child with your physical presence or to shout at him from halfway across the room.

Making eye contact is also very important. If your child tries to look away and run off, hold him by the arms and say: "Look at me please. I am talking to you." Making eye contact tells your child that the issue is serious, and makes him pay attention to what you are saying.

When you are giving a warning or an explanation, use a low, clear, calm, authoritative tone of voice. This tells your child that you mean business, and that his behavior has displeased you. The Voice of Authority is not angry or threatening. It's not uncertain, conversational, or bargaining. It shows your child that you are the disciplinarian.

Q What do you do if your child gets a warning for hitting his brother, but the next time he misbehaves, he does something completely different, like swearing? Should he get a warning for that, too, or do you take him to the Naughty Step straight away?

A That's a good question. Of course, children don't always repeat the same kinds of behavior. They may misbehave in a number of different ways. Misbehavior is the operative word. You need to spell out your house rules – no fighting, no kicking, no swearing . . .

A lot depends on timing. If your son has been warned not to hit his brother and behaves well for the rest of the morning, you can treat that incident as closed. Then, if he acts up later in the day, enough time will have gone by that you can start the process of discipline over again from scratch. In this case, I would warn him not to swear, and wait until he repeats the behavior before putting him on the Naughty Step.

On the other hand, if he has been warned not to hit his brother and then immediately turns around and misbehaves in another way that is unacceptable to you, I would link the two episodes of bad behavior together and take him to the Naughty Step straight away. Some kids will hit, then kick, then bite, for example – you can't apply the technique too rigidly and wait until they repeat the exact same action twice in a row. Try wording the warning in a slightly different way: "You hit your brother. That is unacceptable behavior. We don't hit people because it hurts them. If you misbehave again, you're going to the Naughty Step." Then, when he swears, you can take him straight to the Naughty Step and explain: "You used bad words, and I warned you not to misbehave again. Now, you are going to stay here for X minutes to think about what you've done."

Q *How long should you wait before you take your child to the Naughty Step? Is it a good idea to see if things calm down first?*

A No, you shouldn't wait. As soon as the behavior is repeated, take the child straight to the Naughty Step and sit him down. Sometimes parents delay acting and let the child carry on with the bad behavior until they finally decide it's time to do something. You have to react straight away. If you wait, you teach the child that he can get away with behaving badly for a good while before there's a consequence. Chances are, the bad behavior might even escalate if he's misbehaving to get your attention – what it almost never does is blow over. And before you know it, an episode of toy-snatching has turned into World War Three and your kids are using those toys to hit each other over the head.

There's another reason why you shouldn't wait. Small children don't remember things for very long. Leaving a big gap weakens the association between the discipline and the bad behavior. By the time you get around to acting, he will have forgotten the original incident and protest that you're being unfair.

Q *We've tried the Naughty Step, but it just doesn't work. Our daughter won't stay there for more than a minute. Usually it's less than that. What should we do? Should we hold her in place until she gets the idea?*

A We're all so impatient these days. Many parents turn to these techniques after years of dealing with their kids' bad behavior with no success, and then expect instant results. It takes time.

One of the biggest problems parents have with the Naughty Step occurs when a child refuses to stay put. Let's be realistic here. If your child is not listening in lots of areas, or if a pattern of bad behavior is well established, she's not going to give in without a fight. As soon as you place her on the step, or soon afterward, she's going to get off again and reappear because she's disregarding your authority. It's hard to get some kids to sit down at all under normal circumstances.

In this situation, it is not unusual for parents to quit. Or they may try to restrain their child physically. Neither tactic gives parents the result they want.

So what do you do instead? Reach for the superglue? Bring out the duct tape? Tie her down?

No. What you need is patience, commitment, and perseverance.

You put her back on the step, she gets off, you put her back on the step, she gets off, you put her back on the step, she gets off. Don't start talking to her or show any reaction to the behavior. Simply take her back to the step and place her on it again. Say nothing.

Every time you return her to the step, you demonstrate your consistency, patience, and strength of mind. Eventually she will get it. It might take 10, 11, 12 times the first day. It might take 14, 15, 16 times the next day. But it will work in the end. Trust me, I would know! As long as you follow through, she will stop trying to test you and will accept your authority.

I once had a letter from a mother who wanted to tell me how she had got on with the technique (which she had copied down from the TV). The first day she tried it, she put her child back on the step *100 times*. It took three hours! The next day, she only had to put her child back on the step 10 times. The day after that, it was twice. And every time afterward, her child stayed put. That woman had stamina, and believed that the method would work. She put in the hard work and within three days, she was seeing the results, far quicker than if she had started using the technique, given up, started again, given up . . .

Never attempt to restrain a child when you place her on the step. As soon as you try to hold her in place, she'll fight the restraint. The Naughty-Step Technique is not about overpowering your child physically – that's only a step away from smacking her. If you get involved in this kind of struggle, it could easily turn into a battle. And it is. At the same time, if you force her to sit there using physical means, you show her that you are not confident that the technique will work. Instead, *place* your child on the step. As often as it takes. Do so with an air of confidence and the determination to take charge of the situation. Confidence is like perfume – kids can smell it. So walk it, talk it, and act it.

KEY POINT

Placing a child on the step and returning him to the step when he gets off is the key learning curve within the technique. Place him back every time, and he will see that you mean business. Your authority will be established.

W is for Wisdom.
Wisdom comes from experience and from having the courage to step forward and make mistakes – don't repeat them, learn from them!

Q *Why bother with an explanation? I warn my son and daughter before I put them on the Naughty Step. I don't see why I should go over it all again.*

A The Explanation is just as important as the Warning. Before you leave your child on the Naughty Step, you have to tell him why. Use the Voice of Authority and speak clearly – even if your child is trying to engage with you verbally or is starting to lose it big time. Say: "You kicked your brother. We don't kick anyone – it's not nice."

Why is an explanation necessary? Let's imagine a situation where your two children are playing a board game. Your daughter wins. Your son is so upset he lost that he flies into a rage and throws the game and all the pieces on the floor. You give him a warning. Eventually, after tempers have cooled, your kids settle down and play another game. Your daughter wins again. And your son erupts. This time you take him to the Naughty Step.

Now, quite some time may have passed between the first episode of bad behavior and the second. To make sure your son understands exactly why he is being disciplined, you need to give that Explanation, because teaching him how to behave is your job as a parent. If you don't give an explanation, a child might not know why he is being taken to task and not learn.

Q *How long should a child stay on the Naughty Step?*

A I have a basic rule of thumb: A child stays on the Naughty Step for as many minutes as her age. This is no gimmick, it simply reflects the fact that very little children have short attention spans. A couple of minutes are long enough for a two-year-old. With this age range, consistency and following through are the most important parts of the technique. The amount of time the child spends on the step is important, but it's secondary to the follow-through. When children are older, the increased length of time will have more impact. Eight minutes gives an eight-year-old enough time to calm down and really think about what he's done.

If you are finding it difficult to exert authority or are on the brink of losing control completely, you may be tempted to up the ante. "That's another eight minutes for talking back!" A kid who is sent to a Naughty Room for eight minutes and finds herself stuck there for another eight might as well be serving a life sentence. It's eight minutes, not sixteen or twenty-four. Increasing the time is just moving the goalposts. It undermines the technique and causes frustration all around.

And whatever you do, make sure you're the one in charge of the timekeeping. I introduced the Naughty-Circle Technique in one episode of *Supernanny* to help discipline a three-year-old who was acting up and having tantrums because he was jealous of his sibling. When Ryan's mom Michelle put the technique into practice, she made the mistake of handing him a timer, telling him he could get off the Circle when the time was up, which effectively put him back in control. Of course, the first thing that Ryan did was advance the timer – smart boy!

KEY POINT

If a child keeps getting off the Naughty Step, I usually say that the time should start over each time he is returned there. He must stay put on the step for the correct amount of time before you ask him for an apology.

But . . . I do make exceptions to this rule if there are other factors affecting the child. In the case of a young child who has a short attention span or separation anxiety, or is mentally underdeveloped, I wouldn't do it.

Q *What happens if your child won't apologize? Can she get off the step if the time is up?*

A No, no, no! Parents, whatever you do, don't skip the apology. It's a really crucial part of the technique. It's a resolution. You may well have struggled to get this far – and you may have been returning your child to the step for what feels like hours – but don't be tempted to cut corners here. Your child must say she's sorry. If she is not prepared to say she's sorry, keep her on the step until she does. Go back every now and then and ask for the apology – but not when she calls for you. Return on your own terms. You may have just run a marathon, but don't stop ten yards from the finishing line.

Saying sorry is the last piece of the puzzle because it teaches the child to be accountable for her behavior. It must be a genuine apology. Shouting "SORRY!" or pulling a face while she says it – "Sor-*ree*" – doesn't count. Do bear in mind, however, that small kids sometimes find it hard to articulate clearly. If it sounds like "sorry" to you and she means it, accept it.

Thank your child when she says she's sorry. In that way, you acknowledge her effort. It will have cost her to say it, especially if she's stubborn. It's a major milestone for children to take responsibility for what they do – how many adults still play that blame game? Adjust this technique to an older child; you'll know when an apology is genuine.

The apology also marks the end of the whole episode. It's over. Don't make any mention of what's gone before. Treat the incident as closed, and invite your child to play or join in an activity. Get back on track.

Some parents just can't let it rest. They keep discussing the bad behavior long after the discipline is over. Don't hold grudges.

If your child wants to talk about what's happened, move away from the step before you have the discussion. For example, you might have disciplined your child for fighting over a toy. The discipline will have shown her that fighting for any reason is unacceptable. But say she's still anxious to tell you that the toy is special to her and that's why she got so upset. In that case, you might want to work out a compromise so that the toy is reserved for her own personal use and she isn't expected to share it.

Q What's the difference between a Naughty Step and a Naughty Bench? You seem to use different techniques in different shows. Is there a reason for that?

A Anyone who's watched *Supernanny* will realize that the Naughty Step comes in all shapes and sizes. Sometimes it's a Room, sometimes it's a Point, sometimes it's a Traveling Mat. But it's all the same technique.

Here are some of the variations on the theme I've used on the program:

★ Naughty Circle
★ Naughty Area
★ Naughty Bench
★ Naughty Zone
★ Naughty Room
★ Naughty Chair
★ Naughty Corner
★ Naughty Stool
★ Naughty Beanbag
★ Naughty Block
★ Naughty Point
★ Traveling Naughty Mats

and for those parents who don't like using the word "naughty" –

★ Time Out Area/Space/Room . . .

Whatever you use, the principle remains the same, which is to set aside a specific area where the child must sit out the period of discipline and get ready to apologize. A step is a good place because it's a neutral zone that doesn't offer any distractions, and is not so far removed from the rest of the household that you have to keep running up and down the stairs all the time.

Work with what you've got. In some homes, there are no stairs, so you can't use a Naughty Step. But you may well have chairs, stools, or beanbags you can use instead. You don't have to rush out and buy something special.

If you have more than two children and there's a risk that the child who has misbehaved might pull a disappearing act and vanish upstairs if you put him on the Naughty Step, you may also wish to use something portable like a chair, stool, or beanbag instead. That way you can place it in the room where you are, a little apart from the main area of activity, but close enough that you can keep an eye out if your child gets off the chair before the time is up. I've also used a Naughty Point, which is just a big arrow made out of cardboard that you can stick to the wall.

Sometimes there's the need to discipline more than one child at the same time. In that case, you'll need two or three – or more – of whatever you're using. Naughty Circles and Areas – cheap circular floor mats in plain colors – are a good way of disciplining kids who have been fighting, as you can place the mats at separate points around the room.

A Naughty Bench allows you to place more than one child there at a time.

Make sure the discipline is appropriate for the age of the child. There's no point trying to make a nine-year-old sit on a step or a tiny stool like a four-year-old – it's humiliating. A Room, Zone, or Area works better with this age group. The room or area should offer as little distraction as possible. Taking a child to a Naughty Room full of toys and computer games or where there's a TV is not going to work. Choose a room that isn't her bedroom or playroom and where she can't amuse herself. Porches, lobbies, utility rooms, and dining rooms can be good places. Removing privileges such as video games, pocket money, or not allowing her to go on a sleepover or to a party can also be very effective.

Adapt the technique according to the circumstances. You can't walk around the shopping mall with a Naughty Chair or Stool under your arm, but Naughty Mats or a Naughty Point are easy to carry from place to place. If you're in the playground, use the park bench. If you keep the technique in mind, it goes everywhere with you.

Q *We've tried the Naughty Step, but it didn't really work for our four-year-old son. Do you think that we should change to a Naughty Chair instead? Would that work better?*

A If your son was older, I might advise that you use a Naughty Room instead of a step, but four is still young enough for a step to be appropriate. You don't say why the technique didn't work for you. It may well be that you need to revisit the stages again to make sure you are following through in the right way. If you aren't placing him back on the step each time he comes off it, the technique is not going to work whether you use a step, chair, mat, bench, or something else entirely. If he's backtalking and you're engaging with him, you've got to stop. Put him on the step each time he gets off, walk away, and say nothing.

On one occasion, I visited a family, the Burnetts, who had been using the Naughty Step without success to discipline their three-year-old twins. In this case, the twins often disappeared upstairs when they were placed on the step, and it was too difficult for Mom and Dad to run after them, especially as they had another set of younger twins to look after. So we used a Naughty Chair instead, and placed it in the vicinity of the parents, to enable them to keep an eye out and return their child back to the chair the moment he got off, and at the same time look after their other kids.

While I was teaching the technique, it became clear that there was another reason why it hadn't been working. Mom found it really difficult to follow through, especially when John or Joseph started to cry. As soon as the crying started, she would relent and let them get off the chair. The crying really upset her because she thought that it meant her kids felt ignored by her. She felt like she was being mean, and that her twins would think she didn't love them. What they were doing instead was using their tempers as a means of control. As soon as Mom saw that her kids were happy enough to join in and play after the discipline was over, and didn't hold grudges, she was able to use the technique effectively.

X is for Kisses.
Kids and parents can't get enough of them. Be affectionate and tactile.

Q *I have a four-year-old daughter who has started to behave really badly in public, especially around other kids. I get so embarrassed I just wish the ground would open up and swallow me. I have been using the Naughty Step at home for a while and it works really well, but when we're out at friends' houses or at playgroup, she won't listen to anything I say. If I fuss at her for pushing other children, she just shouts at me. One of my friends is having a birthday party for her daughter next week, and I'm strongly tempted not to go.*

A One word that I hear time and time again from parents is EMBARRASSED, and it really leapt out at me from your question. The way kids behave in public is a real source of concern for many parents. They feel judged as parents when their children act up in full view of other people. You need to address this feeling because it will affect the way you behave when you are out with your daughter.

Most likely one of the reasons your daughter behaves differently in public to the way she does at home is because *you* are behaving differently. Many people are firm at home, but feel inhibited in public, as if Big Brother was watching them. Or they may worry about making a scene. Consistency is the key to discipline. Remember that if you give your child a warning and don't follow it with a consequence when the behavior is repeated, she is bound to ignore what you say – it will simply be an empty threat to her.

When you are out with your daughter and she misbehaves, you can use a **Naughty-Area Technique**. This works in exactly the same way as the Naughty Step. When your daughter pushes her friends, acts aggressively, or misbehaves in some other way, give her a warning first. If she repeats the behavior, take her to the Area, explain why you are placing her there, and tell her you are leaving her there for four minutes while she thinks about her behavior and gets ready to apologize. You can position the Area right in the room where everyone else is playing, but on the sidelines. That way she will be able to see what she is missing by not behaving nicely towards the other children. She will learn that in order to have fun and play, she has to behave a certain way. If she moves off the Area, don't engage with her or discuss her behavior. Continue to take her back there without discussion until she stays put for the required time.

Really stubborn kids often refuse to sit on the Area, but instead sit a few inches beside the area. Provided your daughter is sitting down, don't make an issue of whether or not she's where you asked precisely. OK, for today, it's an Invisible Spot.

Shouting at you is completely unacceptable. The next time she does it, give her a warning, tell her that she is being rude and that if she has something to say, she needs to say it calmly and politely. Follow through with the Naughty Area if she carries on.

Don't be embarrassed or ashamed to discipline your child in front of your friends – if you don't discipline her, they'll only wonder why you don't step up to the plate and get to grips with the situation! Explain what you are doing and they will be sympathetic and supportive. Avoiding social situations might seem a quick way out of your problems, but it won't do you or your daughter any good in the long run. You need to see your friends, and your daughter needs to learn how to interact with other children. Be as firm and consistent with her when you are out as you are when you are at home, and you'll start to see an improvement.

You can also use the technique in other public spaces or situations. Don't worry if other people look at you or attempt to offer you advice. You are the one raising your child, and you aren't the only one who's had to cope with this particular problem. I've used the Naughty Area and Traveling Naughty Mats in lots of different situations with families who were finding it impossible to take their children anywhere without a meltdown, and whose lives were becoming unnecessarily restricted as a result.

If behavior is really spiralling out of control, remove the child from the situation completely. If you're in the mall, for example, go outside and sit on a bench with your child until she calms down and you can try again. Don't flog a dead horse.

And if it's any consolation, I've been on the receiving end of advice myself when a little boy I was looking after for the weekend had a meltdown in public. Despite the fact that this little boy was six years old, he had always been put in his stroller when he went out. I was beside myself – there was no way I was going to take a six-year-old out in a stroller! Before we left the house for the day, I explained that we wouldn't be taking the stroller. I told him about how we were going to go on the red buses and what a good day we were going to have. He was very excited at the prospect. All seemed to be going well until we reached a main road and he had an absolute fit: "I WANT MY STROLLER!" It was a busy road, and I had no choice but to restrain him until he calmed down. While I was doing so, a woman came up to me and said: "Excuse me, but I find Rescue Remedy very helpful." "Thank you very much," I said. Once that little boy realized that his tantrum was not going to change the situation, we had a great day. And I didn't take the woman's advice in a bad way – she was only doing what people do in these situations and trying to help.

Q *How old does a child have to be before you can use the Naughty Step? My toddler, who's eighteen months and into everything, is really driving me nuts. I'm constantly telling him to stop doing something. Help, please!*

A I get asked this question a lot. It all depends on a child's level of maturity. I wouldn't use the Naughty Step on a child as young as yours, unless he is very advanced and coherent in his speech. A child needs to be saying more than a few words or phrases before the technique will work. Once he is talking fairly fluently, you will know that his reasoning is developed enough. In most cases, two is the earliest you can start using these methods.

Getting into everything is what eighteen-month-old toddlers do. It may wind you up, but it's not really a discipline issue at all, is it? Young toddlers love exploring and are even reckless – it's the try-anything stage. Exploring the world is part of the way they learn, and it's healthy. I love it when toddlers squeeze the toothpaste down the drain or bury treasure – obviously you don't want that to be a daily occurrence, but it happens and it shows their busy little brains are well and truly overflowing.

You can save yourself a lot of grief if you keep a step ahead of him. And you'll have to repeat yourself over and over to keep him out of mischief.

Here are a few pointers:

★ **BE REALISTIC** You want a nice home, but don't expect it to be a showcase for the time being. Remove precious items from his reach that he could damage – don't leave that crystal decanter on the low shelf. Cover your sofa with a sheet or blanket that can be thrown in the washing machine – don't waste your energy trying to keep sticky little fingers off the upholstery. Keep a pack of wipes nearby. Washable rugs and curtains are also a good idea. Put childproof locks on cupboard doors where you keep cleaning products, medicine, or chemicals. Be aware of basic safety – put the iron and ironing board away as soon as you've finished with them.

★ **BE ON THE ALERT FOR CLIMBING OPPORTUNITIES** Toddlers love to climb to see all the interesting things that are happening above their heads.

★ **SAFETY** It's a good idea to package wires and power cords into a wire tidy. Watch out for trailing wires – they're invitations to a toddler to pull them to see what's on the other end. Put safety covers into plug sockets. If you don't put your videos away, expect to find the tape pulled out. Some kids will even chew on CDs.

★ **FLASHPOINTS** Be aware of which times in the day are most difficult, and adapt your routine to see if matters improve. If he acts up before lunch, he might be hungry. Bring the meal forward by half an hour. If he's getting into mischief in the evening, he could well be overtired.

Yes, you do need eyes in the back of your head. If you can see trouble brewing, it's much better to steer your toddler away than to take him to task afterwards. Try a distraction – "Let's go see what the cat's doing. Do you think she's sleeping?" Or use the Involvement Technique (page 217) so that you can get on with what you're doing but still give your toddler your attention. If you constantly tell him not to touch, or to stop doing something, he'll quickly pick up on the fact that doing whatever he's doing is a great way of getting your attention. He's not going to stop the behavior when he gets that kind of result.

Q Would you use the Naughty Step for tantrums? My two-year-old daughter has just started to have them and my four-year-old has never stopped. She still has a fit when she doesn't get what she wants. I can't cope with the two of them blowing up every five minutes!

A Would I use the Naughty Step for tantrums? Yes and no.

Tantrums are common between eighteen months and two years, which is why that stage of development is known as the Terrible Twos, although some people say that three can be worse for this kind of behavior. Whichever is the case, nearly every child has erupted in a tantrum before they reach the age of three or four. Some kids have a shorter fuse than others, and tantrums may become a weekly or even daily occurrence for a while.

In young children, tantrums are usually caused by frustration. Toddlers are at the stage where they are developing fast, but their motor skills haven't caught up with what they want to do. Sometimes it's their physical skills that let them down – they want to do something badly, but just can't manage it. Sometimes the frustration comes because they lack the verbal skills to communicate what they want. "Num. Num. NUM!" ("Don't you get it, Mom? I want a banana!") And, of course, kids often have tantrums if you stop them from doing something they want to do, or ask them to do something they don't want to do, especially if you hurry them along. Other reasons include tiredness, emotional upset, and sudden or unexpected changes to the routine.

You can't prevent every tantrum, just as you can't possibly stop a toddler from getting frustrated by the world around her. But you can sometimes spot the signs that a tantrum is heading your way and defuse it before it gets a chance to blow up into a full-scale screaming fit. Use the Involvement Technique (page 217).

It is also very important to give your child a clear warning when another activity is coming up. "We're going to the park in five minutes. Let's go find your boots." Springing an activity on a toddler often causes a meltdown because the child does not have time to prepare for the change. You have to be the Speaking Clock and talk them through their day.

If you can't prevent a tantrum, the golden rule is not to give in to it, which some parents do out of fear. If you give in to a tantrum, you can expect many more where that one came from.

In the case of your two-year-old, this is what I would advise when she has a tantrum:

★ **MAKE SURE SHE CAN'T HURT HERSELF OR ANYONE ELSE** Make sure she can't damage things. Some kids really throw themselves around when they're in the throes of a tantrum.

★ **STAY CALM** Don't get angry, or you will make matters worse. If you can't stay calm and you are sure your daughter is not going to hurt herself, remove yourself from the immediate vicinity and practice some deep breathing (page 192) to get a grip on your temper.

⭐ **DON'T TRY TO REASON WITH HER** She's truly beyond listening.

⭐ **TRY NOT TO RESTRAIN YOUR CHILD** unless she is in real danger. A child in the grips of a major tantrum may well fight the restraint and try to run away.

I would also try to prevent tantrums from happening as far as possible. Pay special attention to the times of day or situations that seem to set her off. Adjust your routine if you suspect she is more likely to have a tantrum before a meal, naptime, or bedtime. Teething and the onset of illness can also trigger tantrums in toddlers.

At the same time, bear in mind that your toddler has a ringside seat at Caesar's Palace when your four-year-old throws her knock-out punches. Small children watch their siblings and copy their behavior, good and bad. When your four-year-old has a tantrum to get what she wants, what happens? Do you give in to her? If you do, your toddler will quickly pick up on the fact that tantrums get results.

In one family, I placed the elder son on the Naughty Area when he threw a fit. At the same time, the younger boy was being disciplined on the Naughty Bench for misbehaving. As soon as the younger one saw his big brother say "sorry," he did the same. Kids learn from each other, and it's not all bad news!

When tantrums or fighting are the main disciplinary issues in children past the toddler stage, I often use a **Reflection Room, Cool-Down Area**, or **Chill-Out Zone**. The technique works in exactly the same way as the Naughty Step. What you are doing is giving your children somewhere to calm down and think about their behavior.

One of the families on *Supernanny* was really struggling with their four-year-old twins. The twins behaved well enough at school, but it was a different matter at home, where tantrums could go on for four hours at a stretch, accompanied by screaming, kicking, biting, and swearing. Neither parent addressed the tantrums. Instead, they tried to defuse them. That might be a good strategy for a toddler who can't help but get exasperated by the world sometimes, but it's a very bad idea when it comes to dealing with an older child who knows exactly what she's doing.

Giving an older child attention for a tantrum is like clapping for a floorshow. It also shows the child that you don't know what to do and can't tackle the problem at its source. Don't put up with it.

In another family, we set up a Cool-Down Area on the front porch. Each time one of their twins lost it or misbehaved, they were warned. Then if they continued to misbehave, they were taken to the Cool-Down Area. They were given an explanation for why they had been put in the Area and told to stay there for four minutes. At the end of the period, they were asked for an apology. All the stages were exactly the same as the Naughty Step, but calling the technique the Cool-Down Area was a way of showing the twins that what their parents were addressing in particular was their temper tantrums.

It took time for the parents to get the hang of the technique. One of the hardest things for either of them to do was to walk away from the Cool-Down Area without engaging further with a kicking, screaming, swearing twin. It was hard for Mom, because once she had got up the courage to confront the behavior, she found it difficult to walk away and let go. It was hard for Dad because he found it difficult to control his feelings of anger. One morning when his daughter was refusing to get dressed and time was running out, Dad abandoned the technique altogether and locked her in her room just so he could get his son into the car for the school run.

It's really important that, once you have given the explanation, you follow through and walk away without saying anything further. Don't rise to the bait, or the tantrum will only escalate and the technique won't work. If you engage with your child while she's in a state of fury, you'll end up with a pantomime on your hands: "Yes you will!" "No I won't!" Yes! NO! Yes! NO! Don't say anything. Give the explanation, then walk away and leave her time to calm down. And just like with the Naughty Step, you have to return your child to the area every time she leaves it, and insist on an apology when the time is up.

One final word of advice: Act promptly. As soon as your four-year-old starts to lash out, discipline her for her behavior. Don't wait until she's had the chance to work herself up into a full-blown screaming fit. It's your responsibility as a parent to implement discipline as soon as your child misbehaves. Don't wait until you've had enough and can't stand it anymore – you'll both be exhausted.

To help this family cope with the anger and frustration they felt when their kids were screaming and out of control, I got them to practice a **Breathing Technique**.

HOW THE TECHNIQUE WORKS

* Breathe in slowly through your nose on a count of five. Imagine you are filling up a big balloon in your belly, from your diaphragm.

* Breathe out slowly through your mouth on a count of five. Breathe out the hot air and flatten that balloon.

* Repeat each time you have to take your child back to the Cool-Down Area.

Q *I have a six-year-old daughter who has been diagnosed with ADHD. She's on medication, but her behavior is very confrontational. What do you advise? We tried the Naughty Room, but it was no real help.*

A In this situation, I would advise a slightly different technique, called **One Strike and You're Out**. Parents who have children with ADHD have to learn the art of compromise. It's important to be aware that you won't be able to control every situation. This technique works slightly differently from the Naughty Room, as ADHD children tend to be very obstinate and persisitent.

HOW THE TECHNIQUE WORKS

★ When your daughter breaks a rule or misbehaves, give her a warning in the usual way, by getting down to her level and making eye contact.

★ If the behavior continues, tell her to go to some other quiet place that offers no distraction, and explain that you will not tolerate her behavior. Tell her that when she is ready to apologize, you will talk to her. These children don't necessarily respond to a set time limit, but be ready to talk once she is set to apologize.

★ As a parent, remain calm and recognize that the important thing is that you must work alongside this medical condition. You can't fight it – you have to bring harmony back to your family life.

★ Carry on with what you were doing, actively praising your other children if they are behaving well.

This technique suits other children who have these kinds of medical conditions. If you actively ignore them when they misbehave, they learn that you will not reward their bad behavior with attention. Keep going with it until she says she's sorry. A child who persistently misbehaves in order to get attention is always pretty thrown when you don't respond the way you usually do.

Q *Toys are a major cause of disruption in our home. We have four boys, aged six to eleven, and there isn't a day that goes by without a fight breaking out over who gets to play with what. They're also pretty destructive, and whatever we give them always seems to wind up broken in no time flat, even the expensive stuff they beg us for. Please help!*

A Toys are often a bone of contention with kids. Boys tend to be more territorial than girls, and toys are one area where disputes often break out. If your boys are consistently behaving badly when it comes to sharing toys – and if they don't respect them enough to take care of them – I would use the **Toy-Confiscation Technique**.

HOW THE TECHNIQUE WORKS

★ Gather all your kids' toys together. Sit your kids down and ask them to choose 10 toys each. Explain that these are the toys they can play with for now. If a toy gets broken, it won't get replaced. Explain that when they have shown that they can play nicely with their toys and each other, they will earn the others back, one at a time.

★ Give each boy a box (color-coded or labeled with his name) and tell him to put his 10 chosen toys in it.

★ Set aside a couple of large boxes for the rest of the toys. Label them TOY CONFISCATION. Ask your boys to help you put the rest of the toys in the confiscation boxes. Remove these from the picture, somewhere where your kids can't get to them.

★ Each time one of your boys misbehaves, remove one toy from his box. When he shows he can behave properly again, the toy can be handed back as a reward for good behavior.

I would use this technique in combination with the Naughty Step (or a variation on the same theme) to teach your children not to behave in an aggressive or destructive manner. And while you are using the Toy-Confiscation Technique, don't buy your children anything new. They have to learn to respect what they already have.

It's also a good idea to teach them in a more positive sense about sharing and how learning to play together nicely means much more fun (see Shared Play, page 219).

Tip: Offside!
If you find yourself constantly refereeing a football match in the living room, make it clear which toys are indoor toys and which are outdoor toys.

The other side of the equation

This chapter has been devoted entirely to ways of disciplining your children by using firm and fair control. What I'd like to say here is that this represents only one side of the equation. I never use discipline on its own. Discipline teaches children that there are consequences to their behavior. Rewards and positive reinforcement teach them how to behave better. Praise, acknowledgment, star charts and other visual aids, treats, and outings are essential to reinforce those occasions when your children behave the way you want them to. The following chapter shows how you can combine positive feedback with firm control to steer your kids in the direction you want them to go.

7 Positive Feedback

Although this chapter is the last in the book, it is by no means the least important. All too often, parents focus on tackling problem areas or dealing with specific types of bad behavior and forget that there is more to parenting than that. Discipline is a key part of raising kids. But so is taking a positive approach to encourage your kids to achieve their own goals in life.

Positive reinforcement through praise, rewards, and shared activities is the other side of the discipline equation. Through positive feedback, you steer your children in the direction of the behavior you want to encourage. At the same time, you build relationships within the family unit and between each child and each parent, making the unit tighter. This is just as important as disciplining your children when they've broken a household rule or crossed the line.

Many of the families I visit on *Supernanny* struggle on several fronts. Behavior has deteriorated to the point where each day is a constant battle, from first thing in the morning to last thing at night. When it gets this bad, it can be difficult to see the light at the end of the tunnel or to find anything positive about family life at all. Parents find themselves uptight, at a low ebb, even depressed. My role is often to point out to exhausted parents who are overwhelmed by the issues they're trying to cope with that there are aspects of their children's behavior that deserve praise and approval, and to show them how encouragement will always have a powerful effect in turning naughty behavior around. Encouraging and rewarding good

behavior gives children the incentive to carry on behaving well. It's all about building self-esteem so they are motivated to continue doing well.

Positive feedback can change the whole family dynamic. It builds trust, respect, and self-esteem – for both parents and their kids. Most important, it brings love and fun back into the picture. And that's what family life should be all about.

Topics and techniques covered in this chapter:

HOW TO PRAISE YOUR CHILD – what to say and how to say it

ONE-TO-ONE TECHNIQUE for individual quality time

THE THOUGHT BOX/VIDEO DIARY to open the lines of communication

HOW TO MAKE A REWARD CHART to encourage good behavior

MAGIC PLAY/ROLE PLAY – family fun to help parents find their inner child

THE PLAY-AND-WALK-AWAY TECHNIQUE – to teach kids to play on their own

THE INVOLVEMENT TECHNIQUE – to keep kids occupied while you get on with things

TEAMWORK – how to teach kids to work and play as a team

THE SHARED-PLAY TECHNIQUE – to teach kids to play together nicely

How to praise your child

Earlier, in the chapter on Family Dynamics (page 10), I talked about the different voices you need to use as a parent when you are communicating with your children. The Voice of Approval is the tone you should use to show your children that you are pleased with their behavior. It's the opposite of the Voice of Authority. Instead of being low and serious, the Voice of Approval is high in pitch and enthusiastic. Many people instinctively go up a register when they talk to babies or small children. This is the same tone you should use to praise your child. You can also use touch to signal approval and reassurance – a pat on the back, a hug and a kiss, a squeeze on the shoulder. Smile! Body language is very important. But adapt your response to the age of your child – a nine-year-old is going to think you're being patronizing if you praise her the way you would praise a toddler. Say: "Well done!" Put warmth in your voice and give her a pat.

"Thank you very much for helping Mommy set the table! Look, you've even put the placemats on!"
"Good boy! You've been waiting very nicely while I got your sister dressed. Now we'll have more time in the park!"
"You behaved very well at Grandma's house, saying please and thank you. Well done! That makes me very proud!"
When you warn your children, you say why you are warning them and identify the bad behavior. It should be the same when you praise them. When your children are doing well, single out the good behavior. Tell your daughter what she did right and how it makes you feel. If you don't identify the good behavior, how will your children know what they're being praised for? Your little boy usually gets up to mischief when you're getting his sister dressed to go out. Today, he sat calmly and played with his train set. You sigh with relief and praise him. "Good boy." If you don't say why, he won't know what he's being praised for – playing with the train set? Getting the train to go all the way around without coming off the track? Making a very good train noise?

Put it in a positive way. Don't say: "I'm pleased you didn't make a fuss while I got your sister dressed today." Say: "You are a good boy for playing nicely and calmly while you waited. That meant I could focus on getting your sister ready. And now we'll have more time in the park." When you explain things this way, you are helping your child to see that his good behavior has a positive result.

Good behavior often goes unmarked by parents. There are several reasons for this. One is that good behavior, especially in small children and toddlers, is often just the absence of bad behavior. Your toddler has given you an easy ride this morning. He's allowed himself to be dressed without a struggle, he's eaten his breakfast without tipping it onto the floor, and he's played happily for fifteen minutes while you sorted the washing. Each and every one of those little accomplishments deserves your attention and approval. If you don't reward good behavior with praise, he'll think you haven't noticed, and he will have no incentive to repeat the performance.

Parents often expect their kids to behave in a certain way, when they have never taught them what they want them to do in the first place. I'm not saying that kids should be constantly rewarded for things they ought to be doing, like saying please and thank you. But if courtesy has been hard for them to learn, and they get it right, they deserve praise. After a couple of weeks, you can let it go and move them on to the next challenge. Every now and then you can remind them of your approval. "May I have another drink, please?" says your daughter. "Yes, you may, because you asked so nicely!"

Some parents don't notice when their kids behave well because they're too busy taking advantage of the peace and quiet to get on with the chores. Some may sense that the day is going smoother than usual, but don't see fit to comment out loud or acknowledge the fact that their kids have made the effort. "Mmm. That was easier than I expected. Sam must have had a better night's sleep last night. Can't last, though," you think to yourself. Or: "Lucy's being a bit quiet. I wonder if she's coming down with something." When your kids behave well, it's not a fluke!

Parents often fall into the trap of only rewarding their kids with their attention when they behave badly. This can be a difficult pattern to break. Kids need their parents' attention, and if they don't get it when they behave well, they will ring all your bells and then some just to get the spotlight trained on them.

It can also be difficult to notice good behavior in one child when another one is acting up. Of course you have to deal with the bad behavior. But you mustn't forget to praise the child who is behaving well – the two of them aren't in the same boat.

Like warnings, praise and approval must be given on the spot for young ones. Don't wait to praise your child – an immediate response will help her associate good behavior with positive attention. With older kids, you can show your approval at intervals throughout the day. And it's always good to revisit the day's highlights later on. When you put your kids to bed, remind them what they did right and how it made you feel. This makes a positive end to the day.

KEY POINT

Paying attention to good behavior and giving your kids praise for it are the most effective rewards you can give.

Tip: One-To-One Technique

On Supernanny *I make sure that parents understand that each child in the family needs one-to-one attention from both Mom and Dad. Individual quality time is very important for every child – it reinforces her sense of herself as a unique person, with her own likes and dislikes, and gives her a chance to develop her personality. I'm not talking about hours and hours out of the house. It's not about the amount of time you spend, it's about being consistent. Work within your routine. And make sure both parents have equal times in their schedules to spend with the kids. Take turns so you aren't stuck in the same roles all the time.*

Q *My mother says that I praise my children too much. She says that if I keep on praising them for every little thing, they're going to be spoiled brats when they grow up.*

A I couldn't disagree more. I don't believe you should ever be stingy with praise. If your children behave well – and that includes just not behaving badly – you should give them your unqualified approval. Many parents reserve praise for the big things their children do well and let the little things go unnoticed. But praise is a very important way of guiding children in the right direction. It's also a key way of boosting a child's self-esteem.

On *Supernanny*, I reward kids when they deal with their behavioral issues successfully. In other words, I reward performance to turn a bad situation around. But sometimes kids make it clear that they are behaving well to get approval and praise. "Look at me! Aren't I being good!" Praise can be much more effective when you reward good behavior that might otherwise have gone unnoticed. Say you've got a friend over and, while you're both talking, your kids are getting on quietly with their play, sharing and taking turns. If you praise them afterwards, that will give them a real glow inside. It will tell them that you noticed and appreciated what they were doing.

Praise doesn't make children conceited, it gives them confidence knowing they're on the right track. A child who is pleased with himself because he has been praised for behaving well or mastering a new task isn't bigheaded. What he's demonstrating instead is competence.

Once I visited a family where a single mom, Kelly, was really struggling with her two kids. Sophie, the eldest, was virtually out of control and had low self-esteem. One day, I complimented Sophie on her beautiful long hair. The next thing that happened was that she asked her mom for hair clips and started trying to put the clips in herself, which she had never done before. Kelly interpreted the fact that her daughter was standing in front of the mirror brushing her hair as vanity. But Sophie was showing that she was competent to take on this task herself, and praise is what had encouraged her.

What is a "spoiled" child? To say something is spoiled is to say that it's ruined. A lot of so-called "spoiled" behavior is a result of parents not setting any boundaries for their kids. Sometimes, it's simply bad manners or rudeness. Or it might be the result of buying kids everything they want and overloading them with material possessions. Teaching children to say "please" and "thank you" and to respect their possessions is always important. But never be stingy with praise; it costs you nothing to give from your heart.

Q *My daughter, who's nine, just won't talk to me. She tells her Dad things, but she won't open up with me. If I ask her how her day at school went, she just says "Fine'" and shuts up like a clam. Then, when her Dad comes home, she chatters away to him about all the things she's been up to. What am I doing wrong? I'm beginning to feel like I don't exist as far as she's concerned.*

A Communication is a two-way street. The fact that your daughter won't talk to you tells me that something has gone wrong with the way she perceives you now.

Parents naturally want to know how their kids have got on during the day, but some kids come home from school and face the Third Degree. "What did you do today? Who did you play with? What did your teacher say about your homework?" Answers like "fine," "dunno," "can't remember" are pretty standard when kids feel like they're facing an inquisition. The questions parents ask often reveal their own anxieties, or have the effect of putting their kids on the hot spot. I sometimes ask kids what made them laugh at school that day – it's a less threatening way of beginning an exchange of news.

How much quality time do you spend with her on your own? You can't put money in a low-interest account and expect much in return. You need to put the time into building your relationship with your daughter. Set aside a regular time in the day when you can be alone with her – watch a TV program together, read a book, play a game, or share an activity, like walking the dog. Get involved with her, and you may find

her volunteering information or initiating a conversation herself once she feels she has the emotional space to do so. Build up the trust and confidence first, and show her that you are interested in her, as a person in her own right.

When I was working with the Doyle family recently, I gave them a quiz. The parents were surprised that I knew more about their children's likes and dislikes than they did. It wasn't mind-reading. I had simply sat down with the two little girls while they got on with their coloring and they naturally opened up and chatted away. I gave them time.

Try giving her a **Thought Box**. Find a small empty box – a tissue box will do – and decorate it. Then give her a special pad and pen and encourage her to write down her thoughts – what makes her happy, what she's enjoyed during the day, and what she hasn't enjoyed or what's upset her. Make a time where you sit down with her and read what she's posted into her Thought Box. I used this technique on *Supernanny* when I visited the Wischmeyer family. The older boy, Jared, had got into the habit of keeping things to himself because he was often unfairly blamed when his younger twin sisters misbehaved. The Thought Box relieved him of his burden of silence and let his mother know how he felt.

If you have a video camera, you could also encourage her to make a **Video Diary**. Set the camera up for her and teach her how to use it. When she has recorded a couple of messages, sit down with her and view the results.

Q *I haven't got much cash to spare. Could you tell me how to make a Reward Chart for my kids like the ones I see on* Supernanny?

A All the charts and other visual aids I use on *Supernanny* are made specially for the families. That's because it's important to suit the reward charts to the age of the children and what they're interested in. Very young children respond well to something simple, bold, and bright; older kids might appreciate a design or picture that appeals to their imaginations or relates to their favorite activities. We use basic materials that are cheap and easily available or that the families already have, like paper and magic markers, storage jars and Legos.

For young children, I like to use **Reward Charts** alongside discipline to help reinforce the good behavior, give a child something to aim for, and provide instant gratification. At the same time, if a child behaves badly, she goes down a place on the chart. With a standard star chart, you award stars or stickers for good behavior. The difference with a Reward Chart is that you also use it to show a child when she has been behaving badly – in other words, she can move down on the chart as well as up.

If you've got two or more kids, each one should have a separate route on the chart – path, ladder, stepping stones – leading to the final goal. Or each child should have her own container, jar, or tower. But if your kids fight or egg each other on when they're misbehaving, and what you're trying to do is to get them to work together in a positive way, use a single chart or tower so that when one child does well, they all benefit, and vice versa.

It's fun to make your own chart and it's not hard to do. Your children will appreciate the efforts you make, and you can always get them to join in with painting and coloring. They also love pictures of themselves.

Here are some ideas to get you started:

★ For the four-year-old Douglas twins whose parents worked at Heathrow Airport, we made a poster of the sky. The sun was what the children were aiming for, and the stepping stones on the way up to the sun were clouds. Each child had a toy plane that could be stuck to a cloud with tape. If a child behaved well, the plane hopped up to the next cloud; if she behaved badly, she was disciplined and the plane dropped down a cloud. When the plane reached the sun, the child got a treat.

★ In the Cooke family, for two girls who loved dressing up, I used a picture of a castle. Each girl was given her own cut-out "princess" (with a picture of her own face on it) who moved up the chart when the child behaved well, and down when she behaved badly. Reaching the castle won her a treat.

★ I used a color-by-number chart for the three girls in the Schwartz family. The picture was a butterfly, and the numbers on the different sections that had to be colored in matched the ages of the girls. Each time a child

behaved well, she was allowed to color in a section of the butterfly that had the same number as her age. When she colored in all her own sections, she was given a reward chosen by her parents.

* Another variation I used in the Facente family was a picture of a gingerbread house with two paths leading to the front door. Each child was given a bear to walk up one of the paths. The bear moved forward one paving stone for good behavior, and back one paving stone for bad behavior. Reaching the front door won a reward.

* For the McMillion family, I used a Reward Chart in the shape of a pie. Each child had their own section of pie and could earn tickets for good behavior, or have tickets taken away for bad behavior. Four tickets equaled one slice of pie on the chart and a small prize. Five slices of pie equaled a bigger prize.

Tip: When a Star Chart is better
A Star Chart is better than a Reward Chart when you are trying to encourage kids to break a bad habit, like bedwetting, but don't want to draw attention to the times they fail. A Star Chart records only the positive behavior, not the negative.

* In the Tsironis family, I used clear plastic containers as **Reward Jars**, one for each child. The jars started off with three Reward Balls already in them. Each time a child behaved well, he got a ball to put in his own Reward Jar. Each time he was placed on the Naughty Point, he had to take a ball out of his Reward Jar. When the child got ten balls in the jar, he was given a reward chosen by the parents.

* A connect-the-dots Reward Chart, like the one I used for the Cantoni family, also motivates kids to work together. Each time one of the kids behaves well, she gets to draw a line from one dot to the next. If one of the kids misbehaves, the line is erased. Once the dots are connected, a picture is revealed and the children get a treat.

* I really went to town with the Wujcik family and came up with a **Reward Box** in the form of a snake pit. We took a cardboard box and decorated it with leaves and jungle patterns. Then we cut a hole in the top of the box and filled it with rubber snakes. Each snake had a tag with a different reward listed on it. Each child was given his own net. When a child behaved well, he was allowed to take a snake out of the pit and put it in his net. When he had won himself four snakes, he was allowed to choose one of them from his net. Whatever it said on the tag was his reward.

You can also use a variation of the Reward Chart to teach children to work together as a team and show responsibility. I used a **Reward Tower** for the three boys in the Young family who were very aggressive, destructive, and disrespectful – and who often encouraged each other in their bad behavior. A ball was removed from the tower when any of the boys misbehaved, and added if one of them behaved well. When they'd managed to get ten balls in the tower, they got a reward. This encouraged them to work together in a positive way. You could make a Reward Tower out of Legos, as we did on another program, and instead of balls use numbered Lego blocks.

Tip: Fun for free

You don't have to spend a fortune to have fun with your kids. Collect old buttons, scraps of ribbon, wool, string or tin foil, cut pictures out of magazines, recycle wrapping paper, empty cereal boxes and toilet rolls, and get creative with scissors and glue. Make pretty keepsake boxes, space rockets, robots, toy animals . . . wherever your imagination takes you. You don't have to beat yourself up trying to earn a scouts badge. Scrapbooking is a hugely popular hobby, and a good way of engaging with your kids. One of the American families I visited gave me my very own Supernanny scrapbook!

Y *is for You.*

Look after yourself and recharge your batteries. If your emotional purse is empty, you'll have nothing to give your kids.

Q *Do you think it is right to reward a seven-year-old with money when he behaves well? I don't see anything wrong with "performance-related pay" for kids, but my wife doesn't agree.*

A The key word in your question is "reward." When is it a reward and when is it a bribe? If you tell your son that you'll pay him if he does such-and-such, sooner or later you're going to have a little stockbroker on your hands negotiating his fee for good behavior. And before the week's out, you're going to see inflation!

What are the best rewards? The ones that get results. Positive attention and praise are essential. Reward systems are good incentives for older kids because they have reached the stage where they have goals. For example, they may want certain material things that they can't afford to buy with their pocket money. On *Supernanny,* I used a reward system based on points (one point equalled 10 cents) when I visited the Pandit family. Jamie, the eldest boy, was a smart kid – smart enough to go on eBay and buy the $70.00 train he wanted using his dad's money and credit card details!

I'm always thrilled to hear when a reward system has been so successful it isn't needed anymore. I've just had feedback from the Cooke family, who were using a Reward Chart to get on top of behavioral issues with their three girls. Denise, the Mom, tells me that she has just taken it down because things are going so smoothly she doesn't need to use it any longer. The kids just trust and know they will be rewarded now.

There are some things your son should just do without expecting to be rewarded for it – keep his own room tidy, and make his bed, for example. A child shouldn't hit the jackpot for doing what he's supposed to be doing anyway. If you over-reward a child for normal behavior, he will quickly learn how to manipulate the situation. "What will you give me if I do what you say?" is not what you want to hear. Then a reward stops being a reward at all and becomes a bribe.

There's nothing wrong with giving a seven-year-old a small weekly allowance to help teach him the meaning of money and what things cost. You can sit down together and write a list of a few toys he would like and show him that, if he saves up his pocket money, he will be able to buy himself one of the things on the list. Make sure the toys on the list aren't too expensive – seven-year-olds can't see far enough into the future to save up for weeks on end! You might also like to pay him small sums for doing extra chores over and above what you expect him to do. But I wouldn't take it too far. Families run better on love and respect than hard cash. He's your son, not your employee.

Tip: Use plastic
If you are making a Reward Chart, cover it with an adhesive plastic or have it laminated (it doesn't cost much). That way you can move cut-out pictures up and down on the chart easily, using tape or something similar. And you'll be able to use the chart again and again.

Q *What kind of rewards should you use in conjunction with a Reward Chart? My girls have more than enough toys already!*

A What do kids want most? Often it isn't the latest toy or gadget, however much they may beg you for it. Instead, it's your time and attention. Parents who are doing their job properly should be giving their kids plenty of time and attention as a matter of course. A lot of bad behavior arises when kids feel they're missing out in this way.

I like to reward kids with outings, games, or special one-to-one time with a parent, rather than material possessions or sweets. I've no great objection to small treats and toys, but time and attention are better rewards and can go a long way toward building good relationships within the family.

What do your girls like doing? What would be a treat for them individually? What would be a treat for your whole family? Small rewards might include a trip to the local swimming pool, fun activities like making cakes or doing arts and crafts, one-to-one attention with Mom or Dad, playing a favorite game or sport. Bigger rewards might be occasions such as a trip to the cinema or a meal out, a day at a theme park, or any activity such as ice-skating or bowling, which you don't necessarily do on a regular basis. These occasions could be enjoyed by the whole family, or provide a chance for one of your girls to have a special time with Mom or Dad.

Q This may sound like a strange question, but how do you play with your kids? My kids are always asking me to play with them, but I can never think of anything to do, and we always end up playing the same board games. I'm getting a little tired of Chutes and Ladders and I'm sure they are, too!

A The short answer is that to have fun with your kids, you have to find your inner child. Bringing out the same board games time after time is . . . boring. That turns play into a routine and a chore. Ask your kids what *they* want to do.

You're not alone. A lot of parents find it difficult to play with their kids. Some parents are too self-conscious to let their hair down and be silly. Some parents regard their kids' playtime as time when they can get on with chores and the adult things they want to do. Some parents use playing games with their kids as the opportunity to compete with them – the Dad who can't let his son beat him at chess, the Mom who's got to win at Monopoly. That just turns play into a stressful situation.

Play is how children learn and how they unwind. Shared play teaches teamwork and cooperation. Playing together as a family strengthens the bonds of love and trust. I always remember my Mom (who was only four foot ten) strapping on a pair of roller skates. All my friends thought she was so cool. She taught us to roller skate backward. She wasn't frightened of acting like a big kid and having fun. She was better at it than us! I remember it like it was yesterday.

So the first thing I would say is to put those board games away for a while and release your inner child. Try some **Magic Play**. I've had parents running around the back garden with sarongs tied around their heads pretending to be pirates, I've encouraged a Dad to sit in a tent in his living room with his boys and blast off to Mars to hunt down aliens... Think of a scenario, get yourself some props or dressing-up clothes, and go with it. It doesn't have to be structured play – let it flow naturally. Just let your imagination run wild, and your kids will have the time of their lives.

Learn to look at the world sideways, the way kids often do. A colander could be a knight's helmet, glitter could be fairy dust, a sheet draped over the sofa makes a perfect cave . . . A game of hide-and-seek is a very simple way of stepping into their world.

Or you could try some **Role Play**. Small kids love to play tea parties or playing house. Or you could be the patient and let your kids nurse you back to health. (You don't need to buy a toy doctor's kit if you don't have one – improvise with some tissues and towels for bandages and an empty toilet-tissue roll or kitchen roll for a stethoscope.)

Play can also be productive and help teach children to concentrate. Spend a quiet hour making things with your kids – string beads to make necklaces and bracelets, make junk models out of old boxes or cartons, or fool around with clay or finger paints. There are many reasonably priced craft kits on the market, and it's easy to pick up the skills.

Q My two oldest kids (a boy and a girl, aged four and six) won't play games by themselves. They always want me to join in. I can't play with them all day – I've got a toddler of eighteen months to look after, too. How do I get them to enjoy themselves for a while without needing to have me there constantly?

A If you haven't done so already, put a structured routine into place. That will help you manage your time more effectively. You have your hands full with your toddler, and there are going to be limited times in the day when you can play with your older kids. Set aside some time when your toddler is asleep where you can focus on the other two. Otherwise, when you need them to get on with things by themselves for a while, try the **Play-and-Walk-Away Technique**.

HOW THE TECHNIQUE WORKS

★ Set your kids up with an activity that they can cope with unsupervised. It doesn't necessarily have to be a game or toy, but don't think about leaving them with art materials that are very messy or tools such as scissors that they might hurt themselves with.

★ Sit down and engage with your kids. Explain how to play the game or do the puzzle or thread the beads on the string. Take a few turns yourself.

★ Once your kids are settled in and comfortable with the activity, walk away and carry on with what you were doing.

★ From time to time, check on the kids while they are playing to let them know that they still have your attention.

Tip: Tell me a story
Storytelling is a great way to bond with your kids. Make up a fantasy world and keep it going over several nights, so your kids are eager for the next installment. Or you could simply tell them what it was like when you were a little girl, or what it was like when Granddad was growing up. Kids love to hear stories about their family history.

Q How do I keep my toddler occupied while I'm looking after our new baby? She's too young to play very long by herself, and I don't like plonking her in front of the video more than I can help it.

A I'm glad you're doing your best to steer clear of using the TV as a babysitter. A good way of trying to make sure your toddler doesn't get irritated by the demands the baby makes on your time is the **Involvement Technique**. This technique is one of my favorites, and works well in lots of different situations. It's especially good with small children and toddlers, but it works with older kids, too.

The basic idea behind the technique is to invite your toddler to join in with what you're doing. Give her a small task or chore to do and keep up a running commentary. "Can you fetch me the plastic spoon? Good girl." "I'm going to wash the carrots for supper now. Why don't you jump up on this stool and pass them to me one at a time. That's a big help to Mommy!" Plenty of praise makes it all go smoothly.

Small children don't make the same kind of distinction between work and play as we do. Instead, they see these kinds of tasks as challenges that they are proud to master. "Helping" Mom and Dad gives them confidence and teaches them to be more independent. Most things are learned through fun.

Obviously, you've got to give your child a task that is within the bounds of what she can achieve, otherwise she will just get frustrated and you may have a tantrum on your hands. Fetching and carrying (within limits – nothing breakable!), setting the table (good for teaching your child how to count), basic wiping down and washing (water play is always fun) are good ways to involve your child with what you're doing. Even a toddler can hold a corner of the blanket for you when you're changing the cover, or help you sort the laundry into light colors and dark, or sweep the floor alongside you with her own mini dustpan and brush. The Involvement Technique is also a good way for Dads to spend time with their kids. Wrap your toddler up in a waterproof jacket and give her a sponge and bucket of water so she can help Dad wash the car.

Be patient. The Involvement Technique may mean that certain chores take longer, and that more mess gets made in the process, but remind yourself that the bonus is that you will get them done without depriving your child of attention and running the risk of her resorting to bad behavior just to get noticed – which will only waste more time in the long run.

This technique is also a good way of heading jealousy off at the pass. A toddler who is involved in the care of her younger sibling gains a real sense of self-worth and responsibility. She'll be less likely to be jealous of the attention you have to pay to the baby when she has a big sister role to play.

Q *My four boys are hugely competitive with each other. Games nearly always end in fights – at the very least sulking and bad moods. Is it too much to expect them to play together without squabbling (they range in age from four to eleven)? We do discipline them when they fight, but it doesn't seem to stop war from breaking out on a regular basis. Is there anything else we could do?*

A A certain amount of competition is healthy. I think it's a shame, for example, when schools rule out competitive games and sports so no one has to lose, or organize activities so that everyone is a winner. Competition encourages kids to aim for goals, and build the steps to success. It's also important to teach kids to be good winners and good losers, and to work as a team to get results. One way they can learn this is through play.

But if games at your house always end in fights, your boys aren't getting the enjoyment from their play that they should. Siblings can be great company for each other. That's an aspect of family life that they're missing out on, too.

What you can do, along with keeping up with the discipline, is to get them involved in an activity that teaches them to work together to achieve a common goal. For the time being, steer them away from games that have winners and losers, and get them to focus on shared activities, both work and play, that teach them how to work as a team. You can also back up the discipline with a Reward Chart or Tower (pages 207 and 210).

Here are some ideas for teaching your children teamwork:

★ Set up an obstacle course using the kids' toys. It can be indoors or outside. Blindfold one child and get the others to guide him around the course just using their voices. The child wearing the blindfold can't move until he's been told where to go by the others. Once he's got around the course, the next boy can have a turn. This kind of activity teaches cooperation, and gets kids focusing on the way they communicate with each other.

★ Treasure hunts are also good for teaching kids teamwork. Write some clues down on pieces of paper. Each clue should refer to a different location inside the house or out in the garden. Don't make the clues too obvious, but don't make them too hard to solve, either. You'll want your four-year-old to have a chance of joining in. Place a reward at the end of the treasure trail and work backwards, positioning the clues at each separate location. Then get your boys to work together to find the clues and reach the reward. Encourage your older boys to help the younger ones and give them plenty of praise when they do. The point is that they should work out the clues together. The reward can be another treasure hunt, or an outing of some kind.

Tip: Pets
Pets are a great way of teaching responsibility and teamwork, as well as nurturing. Kids can clean out the cages, and put in fresh bedding and food and water.

✦ Silly play with water balloons is also good for building relationships. There's no win or lose – the point is to loosen up and have fun. On hot summer days, I used to play water balloons on my bike with my brother Matthew and our friends. It was so much fun.

✦ One of the techniques I also like to use is **Team Clean**. You don't necessarily have to focus on play to build teamwork – shared chores can also do the trick. Choose something that needs cleaning – the car, for example – and gear up the boys with the tools to do the job – you can go over the top and make it fun with bandannas and mops and pails. Assign each child a particular task to suit his age. The little one washes the bumpers, the older one tackles the roof, the middle two wash a side panel each.

Once your kids have shown they can cooperate with each other, go back to the games that were causing the trouble before. Teach them the **Shared-Play Technique**.

HOW THE TECHNIQUE WORKS

✦ Choose a game that all the kids can play.
✦ Sit down with them and explain the rules.
✦ Supervise the game to make sure your kids play fair and take turns.
✦ If they want to go on to play a different game, they have to put the first one away before they can carry on.

The cycle of change

A positive approach is the key to unlocking negative cycles that take the fun out of family life. I have great admiration for all those families who've had the courage to break the mold and unleash their kids' potential through praise and encouragement. You can do it, too.

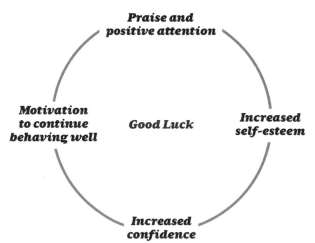

Praise and positive attention

Increased self-esteem

Good Luck

Increased confidence

Motivation to continue behaving well

Z is for Z-z-z-z-z-z. *Sweet dreams!*

Useful Contacts

American Academy of Pediatrics Online
http://www.aap.org — 847-434-4000
General health information on Academy's recommendations and a current events section with up-to-date information on health and safety issues

Autism Society of America
http://www.autism-society.org — 301-657-0881
Includes up-to-date news and information about autism and promotes education and awareness of disorder

Child Care, Inc.
http://www.childcareinc.org — 212-929-7604
Network of referral agencies to help parents find superior child care in their area

Childhelp
http://www.childhelpusa.org — 800-4-A-CHILD
Web site dedicated to the prevention and treatment of child abuse; includes a national hotline

Cure Autism Now Foundation
http://www.cureautismnow.org
888-828-8476
Features information on new treatments and the efforts to find a cure for autism, in addition to providing support for families with autistic children

Crisis Hotlines
http://www.geocities.com/EnchantedForest/2910 /hotlines.html
Provides hotlines for children in crisis

Early Childhood Focus
http://www.earlychildhoodfocus.org
703-341-4100
Up-to-date information on state laws affecting children and child care in addition to general topics including literacy, fatherhood, and special needs children

Family Voices
http://www.familyvoices.org — 888-835-5669
National grassroots organization that compiles information on the care and education of children with special needs

For Parents Only
http://www.forparentsonly.com — 910-493-7861
Search engine with browsers; dedicated to web sites linking research in all areas of parenting, including health, child development, adoption, and pregnancy

Head Start
www.headstartinfo.org — 866-763-6481
Information about child development needs of preschool children for low-income families

Infoparents
http://www.infoparents.com
Interactive web site provides parenting information on key issues

Kidpower
http://www.kidpower.org — 800-467-6997
Non-profit organization offering information on helping kids protect themselves from bullies and adult predators

Kidshape
www.kidshape.com — 888-600-6444
Non-profit organization that helps parents of overweight children create a weight loss management system; increases education and awareness of the dangers of obesity

KidsHealth
www.kidshealth.org
Provides medically approved health info on children, from birth through adolescence

La Leche League International
http://www.lalecheleague.org
1-800-LALECHE
Dedicated to educating and supporting breastfeeding mothers; offers practical advice on physical and emotional aspects of breastfeeding

Learn CPR
www.learncpr.org
A cost-free online course on cardiopulmonary resuscitation

National Adoption Information Clearinghouse
http://naic.acf.hhs.gov — 888-251-0075
Web site features information and support on all areas of adoption for adoptive parents

National Association of School Psychologists
http://www.nasponline.org — 301-657-0270
Articles with advice for parents on how to cope
with crises that affect children in and out of the
scholastic environment

National Down Syndrome Congress
http://www.ndsccenter.org — 800-232-6372
A not-for-profit organization made up of regional
groups designed to advocate for children and
parents dealing with Down syndrome

National Fatherhood Initiative
http://www.fatherhood.org — 301-948-0599
A non-profit organization designed to empower
and increase the number of children growing up
with committed and evolved fathers

**National Organization of
Mothers of Twins Clubs, Inc.**
http://www.nomotc.org — 615-595-0936
Network of more than 400 clubs around the U.S.
devoted to improving public awareness, research,
and private lives of parents of multiples

National PTA
http://www.pta.org — 800-307-4782
National volunteer child-advocacy association
provides information on how to help your child
succeed in school

Parenting Toddlers
www.parentingtoddlers.com
Web site run by a parent of two toddlers with
practical advice and support on raising toddlers;
includes information on discipline, activities,
toilet training, and safety, plus links, blogs, and
message boards

Parents Helping Parents
www.php.com — 408-727-5775
For families of children with special needs

Parents with Disabilities Online
http://www.disabledparents.net
Organization designed to support disabled
caregivers with information on adaptable
products, support groups, and parenting

Postpartum Support International
http://www.postpartum.net — 800-944-4773
A hotline number and support site for women
suffering from postpartum depression

Safer Child, Inc.
http://www.saferchild.org
Provides parents and educators with resources
for any issue relating to pregnancy, childbirth,
child care, and crisis assistance

Single Parents
http://www.parentsworld.com
Articles, advice, and message boards covering all
aspects of single parenting

Stay-at-Home Dads
http://www.slowlane.com — 850-434-2626
Online reference source for fathers who are
primary caretakers in the home

Talk About Twins
http://www.talk-about-twins.com
Parents of twins around the country can post
online questions or requests for twin playgroups
and information

**The National Women's Health
Information Center**
http://www.4woman.gov — 800-994-9662
The federal government's Web site for information
on women's health issues

The Parent Report
http://www.theparentreport.com
Provides visitors with resources and reports on
all aspects of parenting, including healthcare,
single parenting, blended families, family travel,
and discipline; includes links to chat rooms
where parents can help one another with practical
advice as kids grow from birth to teen

U.S. Consumer Product Safety Commission
www.cpsc.gov — 800-638-2772
Information on safety-related issues, including
government guidelines and recall; tips on making
your home child-safe included

**U.S. Department of Health & Human Services
Administration for Children & Families**
http://www.nccic.org — 800-616-2242
Web site dedicated to linking the public with
information about child care

U.S. Department of Health & Human Services
http://www.nccic.org — 800-616-2242
Web site links parents to early care and education
information

Index

abuse, verbal, 39
acceptance, 13
accidents, bowel control, 130
ADHD (Attention Deficit
    Hyperactivity Disorder), 164–5,
    193
Agate, Wendy, 115
aggression, 42, 123, 124
air travel, 140
alarm clocks, 134
allergies, 62, 63
Amaral family, 60, 140
American National Sleep Foundation,
    78
anger management, 124
animals, 218
apologies, 173, 181–2
Asperger's Syndrome, 164
assertiveness, 40
assessment checklist, 15–18
attention, 17
    see also quality time
attention-seeking: at mealtimes, 66, 70
    One Strike and You're Out Technique,
        193
    running off, 136
    shyness, 126, 127
    tantrums, 191
    telling lies, 145
autism, 164

babies: breastfeeding, 61, 64–5
    burping, 65
    crying, 81
    learning to sleep by themselves, 81,
        84, 85
    new arrivals, 38, 156–7
    routines, 21
    sibling rivalry, 124
    sleep patterns, 84–6
    sleeping position, 87
    teething, 64, 81, 91
    weaning, 62–4, 92
baby monitors, 81, 84, 92
babysitters, 119
backtalk, 144
bathtime problems, 133
beds: bed-sharing, 80, 87, 99–101
    moving out of crib, 102
    refusing to stay in, 95–7
bedtimes, 76–107
    routines, 81, 85, 88–9
    suitable times, 20
    see also sleep problems
bedwetting, 81, 94, 95, 104–5
bereavement, 166–7
Big Boy/Big Girl Technique, 131

Bixley family, 139
bladder control, 128–30
blood sugar levels, 54, 74, 75
board games, 215
body language: praise, 202
    warnings, 175
boredom, 140
bottlefeeding, 65, 92
boundaries, 24
    discipline and, 31, 32
    household rules, 110–13, 114–17
bowel control, 128–30
breastfeeding, 61, 64–5, 92
Breathing Technique, 192
bribes, 212
brothers see siblings
Burnett family, 49, 184
burping babies, 65

Cantoni family, 35, 209
car trips, 140
charts: Reward Charts, 207–10,
    212–13
    Star Charts, 209
Chill-Out Chair, 124
Chill-Out Zone, 191
Chimes Technique, 101
choices, 117, 132
chores: encouraging children to do, 147
    Involvement Technique, 217
    sharing with partner, 16, 34–5
    Team Clean, 219
climbing safety, 188
clingy children, 118–21
clothes: faddy dressers, 132
    getting dressed, 131
    potty-training, 129
    Rise and Shine Technique, 134
    twins and multiple births, 50
co-sleeping see beds, bed-sharing
Collins family, 40
communication: with children, 39–41
    family dynamics, 29–41
    household rules, 114
    at mealtimes, 56, 57
    opening lines of, 206
    with partners, 29–31, 35–6
    and routines, 25
    Same Page Technique, 30, 35
competitiveness, 218
confidence: decision-making, 38
    lack of, 81
consistency, 117
Controlled Crying Technique, 90–2
Cooke family, 41, 207, 212
Cool Down Area, 191–2
cooperation, 218–19

crafts, 215
crib death, 87
cribs, moving out of, 102
crises, 150–1, 154
crying: babies, 81
    Controlled Crying Technique, 90–2
    separation anxiety, 118
cycle of change, 219

dark, fear of, 94–5
death: bereavement, 166–7
    crib death, 87
determination, 47
diabetes, 54, 66
diapers, 85, 128, 129
diaries, 14, 15
diet see food
discipline, 17
    communication with partner, 29,
        30–1
    diet and, 54
    household rules, 110–13, 114–17
    mealtimes, 68
    Naughty Step, 32, 170, 172–93
    One-In-Three Technique, 31
    One Strike and You're Out Technique,
        193
    on outings, 138–9
    physical punishment, 32
    step-families, 162
    and telling lies, 145
    Time Out Room, 31
    twins and multiple births, 50
    when not to discipline, 171
distractions, 189
divorce, 46, 160–1
Douglas family, 37–8, 207
Down's Syndrome, 164
Doyle family, 122, 206
dressing see clothes
drinks, 66

early waking, 107
eating see food
eating disorders, 54, 73
eating out, 138
effort, 55
electricity, safety, 188
Elevenish Get Up to Pee Technique,
    95, 105
emotional problems: bereavement,
    166–7
    separation and divorce, 46, 160–1
Everyday Voice, 39–40
exercise, benefits of, 55
explanations, Naughty Step,
    172, 180

extended families, 45
eye contact, warnings, 175

Facente family, 164, 209
faddy dressers, 132
family dynamics, 11–51
  communication, 29–41
  family meetings, 18
  family patterns, 45
  positive feedback and, 200
  routines, 15, 20–7
  single-parent families, 45, 46–8
  twins and multiple births, 49–50
fear: of the dark, 94–5
  sleep problems, 82
  and telling lies, 145
  of water, 133
feedback, positive, 199–219
fighting, 68, 88, 89, 123
flashpoints, 188
food: fussy eaters, 42, 66–7, 69–73
  healthy eating, 54–5
  Little Chef Technique, 60, 72–3
  second helpings, 68
  snacks, 54, 74–5
  weaning, 62–4, 92
frustration, tantrums, 190
fun, 64, 210, 215
fussy eaters, 42, 66–7, 69–73

games, 118, 215
Get Up and Go Chart, 134
giving, 93
goals, 18
good behavior: praise, 202–4
  Reward Charts, 207–10, 212–13
Good Eater Technique, 72
Gorbea family, 34
grandparents, 75
  death of, 166–7
  help from, 48
grief, 166–7
guilt, and sleep problems, 80

hair washing, 133
Harmony family, 120
holidays, 139
home: moving, 152–3
  safety, 188
homework, 147
honesty, 101, 145
housework see chores
humor, 97
hyperactivity, 164–5, 193

illness: families under pressure, 154
  sleep problems, 82, 91

individual attention, 17
inner child, 107, 215
involvement, 105
Involvement Technique, 139, 157, 217

jealousy, 124, 156
journey, parenting as, 113
junk food, 54

kindness, 117
kisses, 184
kitchen safety, 60
Koegel, Dr Lynn, 164

lies, telling, 145
lights, at night, 85, 89, 94
Little Chef Technique, 60, 72–3
love, 118
lying, 145

McMillion family, 209
Magic Dust Technique, 94–5
Magic Play, 215
manners, 40, 56, 57, 123
marriage problems, 160–1
mattresses, safety, 87
mealtimes, 53–75
  discipline, 68
  eating together, 56–7
  fussy eaters, 42, 66–7, 69–73
  Little Chef Technique, 60, 72–3
  routines, 20, 54
Minyon family, 134
money, as a reward, 212
monsters, fear of, 94–5
mood swings, 75
mornings: early waking, 107
  Get Up and Go Chart, 134
  Rise and Shine Technique, 134
moving, 152–3
moving on, after crises, 42–3
multiple births, 49–50

naps, 85, 93
Naughty Area Technique, 186
Naughty Step, 170, 172–93
  age of child, 188
  apologies, 173, 181–2
  consistency of approach, 32
  Cool Down Area, 191–2
  delaying, 177
  explanations, 172, 180
  length of time on, 180–1
  in public, 186–7
  refusal to stay put, 177–8
  special needs children, 193
  and tantrums, 190

variations, 182–3
  warnings, 40, 172, 174–5
nightlights, 89, 94
nightmares, 82, 94
nursery, settling child at, 143
nurturing, 124

obesity, 54
obsessions, faddy dressers, 132
obstacle courses, 218
older parents, 45, 49, 51
Oliver, Jamie, 54
One-In-Three Technique, 31
One Strike and You're Out Technique, 193
One-2-One Technique, 127, 208
outings, 17
  bad behavior, 138–41
  Naughty Step, 186–7
  as rewards, 21
  toilet-training, 130

pain, sleep problems, 81
Pandit family, 212
partners: communication with, 29–31, 35–6
  family dynamics, 16
  separation and divorce, 46, 160–1
  sharing bedtime routine, 89
  step-families, 162–3
  Trading Tasks Technique, 34
peekaboo games, 118
pets, 218
phobias, sleep problems, 82
physical punishment, 32
pillows, safety, 87
Placemat Reward Chart, 72
planning meals, 55
play: Play and Walk Away Technique, 216
  playing with your children, 215
  teamwork, 218–19
  Trust Technique, 135
  see also toys
pocket money, 212
positive feedback, 199–219
potty-training, 128–30
praise, 117, 197, 200
  Big Boy/Big Girl Technique, 131
  how to praise, 202–3
  and "spoiling" children, 204
  Voice of Approval, 40
pregnancy, existing children and, 156–7
promises, 133, 138
punishment see discipline

quality time, 21, 141
  families under pressure, 154
  One-2-One Technique, 127, 208
  opening lines of communication, 206

Reflection Room, 191
regression, 156, 157, 166
relationships: and bed-sharing, 99, 100
  separation and divorce, 46, 160–1
  step-families, 162–3
respect, 144
restaurants, 138
rewards, 17, 197, 200
  money as, 212
  Placemat Reward Chart, 72
  Reward Boxes, 209
  Reward Charts, 207–10, 212–13
  Reward Jars, 209
  Reward Towers, 210
Ririe family, 74
Rise and Shine Technique, 134
Roaming Technique, 136
Role Play, 143, 215
routines, 15, 20–7
  babies, 85
  bedtime, 81, 85, 88–9
  flashpoints, 188
  mealtimes, 20, 54
  new babies, 157
  play and, 216
  special needs children, 164
  twins and multiple births, 49–50
rudeness, 144
rules, 110–13, 114–17
running off, 136

safety: in the home, 60, 188
  sleep, 87
Same Page Technique, 30, 35
sarcasm, 144
school: families under pressure, 154
  homework, 147
  settling child at, 143
Schwartz family, 207–9
security, routines and, 24
self-esteem, praise and, 204
Senior, Debbie, 48
separation and divorce, 46, 160–1
separation anxiety, 118–21
Separation Technique, 120
sharing, 145
  bed-sharing, 80, 87, 99–101
  Sharing Bins Technique, 123
  toys, 122–3, 195
shopping: bad behavior, 138
  Involvement Technique, 139
  shopping malls, 139

shows, bad behavior at, 139
shyness, 126–7
siblings: fighting, 68, 88, 89, 123
  new babies, 38, 156–7
  playing together, 218–19
  rivalry, 124
SIDS (crib death), 87
single-parent families, 45, 46–8, 100–1
sisters see siblings
sleep and sleep problems, 55, 78–107
  babies, 84–6
  bed-sharing, 99–101
  bedwetting, 104–5
  Controlled Crying Technique, 90–2
  deep sleep, 83
  early waking, 107
  learning to initiate, 65, 81, 84, 85, 99
  moving into a big bed, 102
  naps, 85, 93
  safety, 87
  Sleep Separation Technique, 102–3
sleeping in, 107
smacking, 32
smoking, and crib death, 87
snacks, 54, 74–5
  Snack Jar Technique, 74
soiling, 130
special needs children, 164–5, 193
"spoiled" children, 204
Star Charts, 209
step-families, 45, 162–3
Step Up/Step Back Technique, 35
STOP signs, 136
storytelling, 216
strollers, 136
sugar rush, 74, 75
supermarkets, 138, 139
support systems, 18
  crises, 150
  single-parent families, 47
  twins and multiple births, 50
swaddling, 87
swearing, 117

table manners, 56, 57
Talking Stick, 57
tantrums, 81, 190–1
Team Clean, 219
teamwork, 218–19
teething, 64, 81, 91
television, 56, 57, 68, 89
temper: parent losing, 40
  tantrums, 81, 190–1
Thought Box, 206
time management, 20–7, 153
Time Out see Naughty Step
Time Out Room, 31

Timer Technique, 122
tiredness, 78–9, 80
toilet-training, 128–30
toilets: seats, 129
  using at night, 95, 105
tone of voice see voice
toys: saving up for, 212
  sharing, 122–3, 195
  Toy Confiscation Technique, 195
Trading Tasks Technique, 34
travel: car trips, 140
  sleep problems, 82
  see also outings
Traveling Naughty Mat, 138
treasure hunts, 218
treats, 213
triplets, 49–50
Trust Technique, 135
Tsironis family, 42, 145, 209
TV, 56, 57, 68, 89
twins, 49–50

values, 171
vegetables, fussy eaters, 69
verbal abuse, 39
Video Diaries, 206
voice, tone of, 39–40
  Everyday Voice, 39–40
  Voice of Approval, 40, 202
  Voice of Authority, 40, 175, 180

warnings: Naughty Step, 40, 172, 174–5
  One Strike and You're Out Technique, 193
  preventing tantrums, 190
  and routines, 25
washing hair, 133
water, fear of, 133
water balloons, 219
weaning, 62–4, 92
Webb family, 164, 165
whining, 127
Wischmeyer family, 206
wisdom, 178
working parents: routines, 26
  and sleep problems, 80
Wujcik family, 209

Young family, 32, 36, 57, 74, 210
yourself, looking after, 210